The Original

THE ORIGINAL
Living Life Through Hockey

Written by
NORM BEAUDIN
with KIM PASSANTE

Edited by
STACY PADULA

Foreword by
PETER YOUNG

Briley & Baxter Publications | Plymouth, Massachusetts

ISBN: 978-1-954819-49-8

Book Design: Amy Deyerle-Smith

In Loving Memory of Linda Beaudin
(April 2, 1944-May 17, 2021)

TABLE OF CONTENTS

While this book was in the process of being published, Norm Beaudin's wife, Linda, passed away on May 17, 2021. Linda had a legendary sense of humor and a tremendous matriarchal way about her, and although the disease of Alzheimer's took hold the past few years and dementia removed many of her faculties, she continued to sparkle right to the very end.

Linda was born on April 2, 1944 and was raised in Regina, Saskatchewan as an only child. Her loving parents Eunice and William (Bus) Lowes gave her a beautiful upbringing with many friends and family vacations to Vancouver. While Linda was studying nursing at Regina College, she met the love of her life, Norman Beaudin, an up-and-coming hockey star with the Regina Pats. They married in 1962, and for almost two decades Linda lived the life of a Hockey Wife, and was the glue that held the family together.

Linda and Norm crisscrossed their way through iconic hockey cities across North America, with stops in Ottawa-Hull, Indianapolis, Cincinnati, Pittsburgh, Memphis, St. Louis, Kansas City, Buffalo, Ft. Erie, Cleveland, Minneapolis and Winnipeg, then off to Langnau and Sierre, Switzerland for a European adventure. Linda would reel Norm back home to Regina for family support in the off-season before making Winnipeg their permanent home in 1972, where they formed a solid base of life-long friendships. From 1976 to 1979, Linda took a leap of faith to support Norm while he pursued a player-coach role in the Swiss Elite Hockey league. It was in Switzerland that Linda learned to speak German and became a pillar of the community with the American embassy and International School of Berne families, as well as the local Catholic church parishioners. Moving a family of six to live in a small German-speaking farming town could not have been easy, and yet Linda made it all work with a can-do, breezy attitude. She always made the role of wife and mom appear effortless and easy, as she trekked across the continent with 1, 2, 3, then 4 kids in tow. Always quick to make friends in new places, Linda had a feisty superpower in the way of playing Bridge, which helped her to establish roots wherever she landed.

Upon returning to Winnipeg after three full years in Switzerland, Linda revved up her work career as an office administrator at the bustling Silver Heights Medical Clinic. After many cold winters and with the kids grown up, in 1988 Linda and Norm made the big move to Clearwater, Florida.

Linda's humor, strength, and resiliency always softened the impact of any stress and struggle that came from moving around. She worked in the medical profession, assisting various groups of doctors with her administrative wizardry in Winnipeg and Florida. She then took over the financial management of the Beaudin's Hockey Zone and Skate Shops, always ensuring stability behind the scenes while making sure to be the entertainer and hostess at the front of house, and in the rink, with hard work and laughter always in the mix. Linda took the role of Hockey Mom to a whole community at the Tampa Bay Skating Academy and JP Igloo Arena in Ellenton. She made many friends inside the rink, and probably never really watched a full game, from end to end, ever! Never one to watch the scoreboard or care who won or lost, Linda was all about the people she was with, making everyone laugh and feel special. Linda's faith and fortitude were tested to the max when daughter Carrie-Lynn suffered a ruptured brain aneurysm in 1996. Shortly thereafter, however, a miracle and blessing appeared in the form of a call, with a very special person on the other end: her birth mother Christine McGrath from Enderby, BC who had given Linda up for adoption during the war years. They were both keen to meet and a reunion plan was hatched. This led Linda to meet her bonus family of TEN brothers and sisters that she never knew she had, completing her spiritually in a way that was always missing in her life. Linda's new family all became quick friends and shared many tremendous memories.

Linda and Norm left Florida in 2013 for a new adventure in Scottsdale, Arizona where, again, she would build an amazing group of new friends through entertaining, cards, and trips to the hockey rink with Norm. It was in Arizona when the Alzheimer's disease began to surface and that would lead to a move back to Canada in 2017 to be closer to their family in Vancouver, Carrie-Lynn, Greg, Odette and Celeste.

Linda was the cherished mother and adored grandmother of David (Brooke & David Jr.), Nadine (Eva), Greg (Odette & Celeste) and Carrie-Lynn. Linda was also embraced as Daughter in-law to Martial and Ferdinand Beaudin (both deceased), Sister in-law to Alain Beaudin (deceased), Harvey and Jeannette Beaudin (both deceased), Lorraine and Jim Wasser (both deceased), Edwin and Diane Beaudin, Annette and John(deceased) Kaufman, Claude(deceased) and Rose Beaudin, France and Ted Theoret, Leona and Ed Thevenot (deceased), Jocelyne and Tom Williams, Aurel and Sandy Beaudin, Bob and Eunice Beaudin.

Linda truly loved being the new daughter to Christine McGrath "Mom" (deceased), and beloved sister to; Alvin (Butch) and Pat McGrath, Donna and Reg Newman, Victor and Barb McGrath, Victoria and Bob Walker, Marlene and Bill Redding, Max McGrath, Donalda and Doc Taylor Danny and Linda McGrath, Maryanne Litzenberger, Bonnie and Patrick Skelly.

She was an adored Aunt to many Beaudin and McGrath Nieces and Nephews and Linda was also loved by the Lowes and McMinn families who were instrumental in her upbringing. The Beaudin family would like to thank all the wonderful caregivers at Capilano Care Facility (Special Care Unit) and Evergreen House, where she spent her final days.

FOREWORD

I've met thousands of athletes over a twenty-five-year career on national television in Canada. I've been behind the microphone and in front of the camera for multiple Olympic Games, World Championships, International Tennis Tournaments, Grey Cups, F1, and Indy Car races. And I've be fortunate enough to handle television play-by-play duties in the Canadian Football League, the National Hockey League, and International Hockey. After calling radio play-by-play since I was a teen, my first major league foray into the television broadcast booth was in the World Hockey Association. Valentine's day, 1975, Bobby Hull and his Winnipeg Jets against Gordie Howe and the Houston Aeros. All those years broadcasting junior and senior hockey in the Lakehead and suddenly I'm calling a game featuring two of the greatest players of all time. Also on the ice in that game, Hull's linemate for the first two seasons in the WHA—a man who would become a lifelong friend: Norm Beaudin. What an honor to be asked to write the foreword for this book.

You could probably blame the late Billy Robinson, the late Don Baizley, or the late Dr. Gerry Wilson. Norm Beaudin would have likely finished his North American pro career playing alongside legendary Bobby Hull were it not for those three Winnipeggers. In 1973, the Winnipeg Jets executive (Robinson) asked the former Montreal Canadien (Wilson) to scout some Swedish first division games while he was studying orthopedics at a sports institute in Stockholm. If Wilson had turned down that opportunity he would have never discovered talented Swedes Ulf Nilsson, Anders Hedberg, and Lars-Eric Sjoberg.

The respected lawyer and player agent, Baizley, would have never negotiated contracts for the three stars to join the Winnipeg Jets for the third season of the World Hockey Association. The greatest line to ever play in the WHA, or maybe all of hockey, Hull-Hedberg-Nilsson, would have never been formed. And Beaudin, Chris Bordeleau, and the Golden Jet would have had a few more productive seasons in Winnipeg.

Beaudin was the first player signed by Ben Hatskin before the Winnipeg businessman shocked the hockey world by luring Hull from the Chicago Blackhawks in 1972, pretty much giving the upstart league instant credibility. A junior hockey superstar with the Regina Pats, Beaudin had played parts of two seasons in the NHL with the St. Louis Blues and Minnesota North Stars and came to Winnipeg after a thirty-three goal, thirty-three assist season in the American League with the Cleveland Barons. He was immediately put on a line with two former Blackhawks teammates, Hull and Chris Bordeleau, and they clicked out of the gate. The "Luxury line" led the Jets for two seasons with the native of Montmartre, Saskatchewan scoring thirty-eight goals and adding sixty-five assists to lead the Jets in scoring in their first season. All three players on that line recorded 100 point seasons that year, a first in professional hockey. I didn't get to see any of those heroics in person, but as a young sports broadcaster in Thunder Bay, Ontario, I certainly followed the Jets.

When I moved to CTV in Winnipeg in 1974, Norm was one of the first Jets I met, and I've been able to call him a great friend over the past forty-seven years. I was fortunate enough to cover the Jets on their successful 1975 European training camp in Finland, Sweden, and Czechoslovakia—one of great team bonding events in their history.

With the arrival of Hedberg and Nilsson, Norm's role on the Jets changed dramatically. The Swedes and Bobby got ninety percent of the powerplay time and first-line minutes, but Beaudin found other ways to contribute. As a premier penalty killer, he became a shutdown forward often playing against the opposing team's best players but still contributed thirty-two goals and ninety-four assists over the next two seasons. Loved and respected by his teammates, he was named assistant captain after the Swedes and Finns arrived. After four incredible seasons with the Jets, Norm was finally able to hoist the AVCO Cup before putting an end to his playing career in North America.

Thankfully, we've remained friends for almost half a century, through his days running a golf course in Apollo Beach, Florida, numerous Jets Alumni events and reunions, and Pond King charity games. I also became great friends with his sons Dave and Greg. In fact, Dave and I were roomies for a while in St. Pete, Florida. Norm and Linda relocated to Vancouver to be closer to Greg and their daughter Carrie, and he's finally managed to find time to put his incredible life and career into this book. I hope you enjoy it.

Peter Young
Former CTV & WHA Winnipeg Jets TV play-by-play broadcaster

PREFACE

RED LIGHTS FLASHING!!! SIRENS BLARING!!! Things you see and hear when a goal is scored.

Only there was no game. No, these were the sights and sounds reverberating through my head as my daughter asked me if she could go out with a hockey player—a goalie, no less.

And so it happened. It was a beautiful Arizona weekend and a group of us were gathered in the restaurant at the Ice Den Scottsdale. A group of hockey players and their true home teams: their spouses, significant others, and children. I was being thrust into the world of hockey, surrounded by it on all sides. The Den seemed to be our second home, as my daughter was constantly figure skating and my husband had started playing with some retired NHL players whom I had never heard of. Come to think of it, at the time, I really couldn't name more than two hockey players at all—neither one of them with the initials NB.

I had no idea that sitting there amongst our group was such an amazing couple, Norm and Linda Beaudin, who in time we would come to grow very close to, traveling together and embarking on this journey to share Norm's story with the world. At the time, all I knew was that my daughter was no less excited than a home crowd watching a game-winning puck slide between the pipes and tickle the twine behind the visiting team's goal tender. Her eyes lit with fourteen-year-old excitement, no dimmer than the way the lamp behind the goal flashes along with the spotlights in the arena as the home team scores.

And no more let down was I than that of the losing net minder. Having the youngest of my children, my precious baby, the caboose of the family, want to date a hockey player conjured up all kinds of petrifying thoughts in my mind. I was the goal tender, protecting her from all things dangerous, craftily deflecting danger as it sped her way; yet here, on my watch, she was wanting to venture into the world of dating with none other than a hockey player.

In lamenting the situation to our tablemates, I was extremely surprised to hear from this seemingly wise and well-experienced pair that a hockey player could indeed be an ideal choice for a date. Norm explained how a dedicated, top-tier athlete like a hockey player must have great personal strength and good character to do what it takes to reach and remain at a highly-competitive level. Norm and Linda went on to extol the virtues of well-principled hockey players with whom they have been friends for decades. With their excitement for the game, their argument won me over, and I consented to a supervised first date with the goalie. Supervised—by her dad and me... and maybe Norm... and perhaps a half-dozen or so other big, burly hockey players who knew and looked out for her.

At the time, I was new to this sport and showed my obvious naiveté like a little kid at his first hockey lesson, schlepping over their shoulder one of those giant wheel-less gear bags while looking for the locker room. It seemed I was regularly lost in a sea of game-day talk rife with testosterone, energy, excitement, confidence, defeat, analytics, the usual.

Despite trying to get into watching hockey in the nineties, I had yet to catch the bug. My first viewings of televised hockey had left me frustrated, as I found tracking the puck nearly impossible and just couldn't get my mind into watching something that revolved around all things cold. Years earlier, I had moved to the desert to escape the snow country, and here I found myself regularly sitting next to a sheet of ice. I do, however, admit to having a year-round, very close relationship with all of my winter clothes and a large stock of disposable hand warmers. Yes, we live in Scottsdale, Arizona, but I regularly use the heated seats and steering wheel in my car after a long session in the rink, as I suppose many more do than will admit.

Times changed, as times do, however, and the NHL has definitely upped its game. Players are more accessible, the television coverage is much better than in the past, and with HD television, viewers can easily track the puck as it flies across the ice. We are able to watch our teams practice, and they work well within their respective communities to help kids who are interested in playing the wonderful game of hockey. Girls leagues are growing in popularity across the nation, and Norm definitely inspires those he comes to meet.

In getting to know Norm, it became obvious that he was a natural for sharing his stories and experience and that he needed to share those with as broad an audience as possible—thus this book was born. Norm is one of those people who lives by the credo that everyone has a story and that story is worth sharing. He and Linda love to hear the stories of others, the backstories. They are kind, compassionate, and caring as few others I have met. They listen patiently as their friends and compatriots converse with them—be they family, longtime friends, or newfound acquaintances.

Norm is never the first in a group to tell a story; he always listens to everyone else first. He gives advice by listening, then telling one of his related stories from his vast life experience. Norm's story is not *about* hockey but *through* hockey.

Hockey has not only given Norm many opportunities to help others, but also prepared him in so many ways for life's challenges. On the ice, one must be ridiculously adaptable, play at breakneck speed, yet remain patient, distinguish friend from foe, evaluate all possible outcomes of each play, be able to identify and handle potential conflicts, and have the courage to initiate the next move. If that doesn't prepare someone well for life, I don't know what does.

Along this path of meeting not only great hockey players, but also individuals involved in the sport at all levels, I can say that I haven't met or heard of a greater advocate for the game of hockey—for a life of hockey—than Norm. I haven't met anyone who knows him and doesn't love him. He's not pretentious or arrogant, and he always carries himself as a gentleman. He lives to get to know others and to help them in any way he can. The world is definitely a better place because he is in it.

Kim Passante

INTRODUCTION

Several years ago in 2013, when I moved to Arizona, the first place I was attracted to, naturally, was an ice rink. Wherever I go, be it Florida or even the desert of the southwestern United States, I can't seem to manage being away from the ice for any serious length of time. So, I hunted down the nearest rink, which was the Ice Den in Scottdale, and walked in to meet the staff. The first person I met was the president of Coyotes Ice organization, Michael O'Hearn. Interestingly, I knew Michael from Winnipeg, and this seemed to be a perfect fit for me. My first question was if they had an adult hockey clinic, which they did not. I subsequently spoke with the hockey director, Becky Conlon, and we decided to put something together.

The clinic was a success from the beginning, attracting twenty-five to thirty skaters every Friday. Friends were made right from the beginning, with one gentleman in particular: a young man named John Passante with whom I grew to be great friends. I started playing in a league there and got to play on John's team. Our friendship outside of the rink grew as well, with Linda and I meeting John's wife, children, parents, and brother. Over the years, we spent most holidays together, enjoying Christmas and Thanksgiving dinners together, as well as many parties. We would sit around and share our respective stories, and repeatedly, people would tell us that I needed to write a book about my life and career. Never being one to shy away from a new venture or project, this book was born.

After the urging of many friends, with the writing of this book, I want to let the world and all the sports people know what it takes to play professional sports and share with them the great trials and tribulations we went through in the early years of this sport. It's not all as glamorous as some would wish it to be, yet at the same time, it is incredibly rewarding. I will depict exactly how a young person had to fight the establishment at every level and highlight some controversies that may be considered taboo, even after all these years.

This book will also emphasize how important an education is to all young persons and especially to any aspiring young athlete, no matter what the sport. Without your education, a great deal of your bargaining power is gone, as well as post-play opportunities, and as you read this book, you will understand. So, play your sports but don't skip your education.

Enjoy the book, enjoy life, and happy reading!

PROFESSIONAL CAREER

Eight leagues
Saskatchewan Junior Hockey League
Western Hockey League
Eastern Professional Hockey League
American Hockey League
Central Hockey League
National Hockey League
World Hockey Association
International Competition

Fifteen teams
Regina Pats
Spokane Comets
Hull-Ottawa Canadiens
Pittsburgh Hornets
Indianapolis Capitols / Cincinnati Wings
Memphis Wings
Kansas City Blues
St. Louis Blues
Buffalo Bisons
Cleveland Barons
Minnesota North Stars
Winnipeg Jets
Switzerland Langnau Tigers
Switzerland Sierre Siders

"NO WORDS"
BY KIM PASSANTE

There are no words to describe the sound an elite skater hears as
the cold steel blade carves its signature into the frozen sheet beneath them
Tiny crisp snowflakes,
Beautiful, sparkling crystals of ice
Rise up in a shimmering mist then gently fall back to take their place on the serene
surface
There are no words
No words to describe the elation a skater feels
when the attention needed to traverse the ice while remaining vertical fades into
the background and
the skills needed to perform as an athlete move to the forefront, demanding full
focus
From then on, cues are taken from that very sound
The condition of the ice
The temperature of the sheet
The sharpness of the metal edges upon which the skater relies
The force behind each stride
The flexibility of the knees
The stability of the ankles
The strength of the muscles working in harmony
The energy immediately available and
The reserve upon which they have to draw,
All identifiable to the skater with each stroke

There are no words
For that sound that drowns out all others
The harmonious beat and melody
A tune that leaves no other worthy of comparison
Like the scythe that carves swaths of wheaten bounty,
leaving behind a clean, evidentiary vestige,
a record of the moment captured, albeit temporarily
A record that, while momentarily obvious,
Is etched briefly into the skater's mind, into their psyche, but
will all too soon fade into nothing more than an aging snapshot,
a dissipating record of that place in time,
replaced by its contemporary
That sound that gathers data
Feeds the soul
Focuses the mind
Transports the skater into their zone
There are no words
Just
The Sound

ACKNOWLEDGEMENTS

The clock shows five in the morning, I'm sitting in the lobby of the Hilton Ballpark Inn in St. Louis, reflecting on the past fifty years. At my age, sleeping past four or five a.m. doesn't seem possible. It's in my DNA, I suppose, being from the farm; it seems that is always instilled in our body. Having just wrapped up a fiftieth anniversary celebration with the St. Louis Blues, I marvel at how many people I have to thank for giving me the material to write this book and the ability to share my experiences with an audience in this way. I have indeed had a great life.

Parents and siblings

Firstly, I need to thank my family. My parents, without whom I wouldn't be here physically, mentally, or spiritually, and my siblings for being a body of strength throughout not only my hockey career, but my entire life. I would like to make note and embrace the good times that we spent together. At different times of our lives, we didn't spend that much time together because the older ones would leave home and the young would take over. Although that was happening, we always cared for each other. I don't remember having any malice toward each other. We always tried to help each other when needed and could always depend on one another. We did not go around saying "I love you." We showed our devotion through our actions.

I am thankful for the devotion that my parents held toward all their children and family. They worked very hard sheltering, feeding us, and giving us direction. As a family we were so far apart in some ways but so close when we did get together. It was like we had never been apart. That certainly reflected on Martial and Fernande Beaudin. To me, they are saints in their own right. Rest in peace.

Wife and children

I would like to thank my wife Linda for her contributions to this project. We've been working on this for years, and she remembered a lot of the dates that are relevant for this book and different incidents that occurred during our married life. Unfortunately, she now suffers from dementia and will not be able to enjoy reading these pages and the fruits of our efforts, but without her, this would not be possible.

I would like to acknowledge all my children Dave, Nadine, Gregory, and Carrie Lynn. Carrie, who is wheelchair bound, is such an inspiration, living life with a very positive attitude, showing us how to be strong and not quit. I thank all of them for the data they provided.

Hockey mates

Throughout my life, I have been privileged to meet so many wonderful people, mostly through the game of hockey, and our friendships have transcended the game for decades now and hopefully for decades to come.

Thanks to the Winnipeg Jets and Ben Hatskin for believing in the WHA and making it thrive.

Thanks to Bobby Hull for without him this book would not have happened.

Thanks to Joe Daley, a teammate and certainly a good family friend who was instrumental in getting me information that I needed to write this book. Thanks to AB McDonald for being our first Captain for the Jets and being our strong leader.

The WHA

A great and humble thank you goes to the WHA and those brave and innovative souls who founded the new league and grew it into the successful organization that it became. Thank you from the bottom of my heart!

NHL and the fans

As far as the impetus for this book, I owe all that to the sport of hockey, the pinnacle organization, the NHL, supporting staff, its precursors, the players, and the loyal and devoted fans and communities. Thank you, thank you, thank you. Without all of you, we wouldn't be taking the ice and sharing the game we love with all of you, our wonderful worldwide family. Special mention to the original Winnipeg Jets fans for the great support that was bestowed upon us and for embracing the new Jets team. Thank you also to the St. Louis fans from years ago and today's fans for being so gracious when we went back for the fiftieth anniversary celebration. How magical it was to be on the ice in St. Louis once again and what an honor. Thank you.

Beyond the Ice

Thanks to Ted Foreman for being my financial advisor and a friend of the family, and for getting me a job after I retired. Thank you as well to Peter Young for taking my calls for data that I needed. Your help is greatly appreciated. And lastly, thank you to everyone not included above, as I feel friendship in the world around as I travel and hope you enjoy my stories as I have penned them down for you to peruse.

Merci to all of you,
Norm

Disclaimer
The names, events, and stories included herein are to the best of my recollection and any inaccuracies including misspellings are purely unintentional.
~ Norm

Chapter One

A HOCKEY PLAYER IS BORN

It was a cold day, I'm told. The coldest day in memory for my uncle. Fifty degrees below zero he would say that November 28, 1941, in Montmartre, Saskatchewan, Canada—the day I was born. Many a time have I heard about how my mom almost died birthing me. They actually gave her the last rites, thinking she wouldn't make it through, but pull through she did, and she lived to give birth to many more. Sometimes I would hear from people that I was her favorite, and while I never wanted to be favored over any of my siblings, I wonder if perhaps I was. Maybe she was thankful that we had pulled through together or perhaps she was scared of me? I don't know, but it seems things worked out in my favor. Whatever the influences were, I seemed to slide straight from birth into hockey skates and haven't hung them up to this day.

I came to learn early on that in the game of hockey, sometimes we get where we're going because of things we *do* control and sometimes because of things we *don't* control. There are times when we win using tactful diplomacy, sometimes by the clever manipulation of organized rules, sometimes simply because of a lucky flip of the puck, or a variety of other such factors. And sometimes, it's just because you want it more than anyone else and you just physically outdo your competitors. It is in life as it is in hockey.

Many of my early days skating could be summed up by those last sentences, and undoubtedly, my siblings would agree—especially two of my sisters, who for a while wore the same size skate as me. Unfortunately (for them, usually), in our world of limited resources and hand-me-downs, that meant only one of the three of us got to skate at a time. As much as I had been taught to be fair and tactfully diplomatic, *fair*

1

is, to be honest, a relative term. To me, it was *fair* that I got first shot at those skates until I grew into the next bigger pair. It was I, who loved hockey with every cell in my body, who *should* wear those skates. Sure, I was occasionally hit with a bout of conscience—and perhaps the tap of an elder's stick—and relinquished control of the skates to the girls for a turn, but I was a kid, and a kid with a passion, and it only seemed fair that those skates were on my feet.

In talking to my sisters in our later years, I have realized that my parents did show preference for the boys in our family. My sisters would cook the meals and make sure we would all be fed, and once our bellies were full, we boys would naturally take off and the girls were left to clean up and finish the chores that we did not do. My poor sisters would pick up the slack receiving no thank-yous or even a goodbye. Now that we talk about it, my sisters certainly were begrudged at the time, but now we can laugh about it. It helped me a lot that they were there to do all that work. Once I learned things from their perspective, I tried to make it up to them. Sorry about that, sisters!

Being born in Canada gives one a good start in the field of hockey. Hockey blood seems to course through the veins of nearly all Canadians and even though I was the ninth of thirteen children born to a family of limited means, we had a closet full of skates and sticks. We may not have had the best of gear, but we made do with what we had. We also learned to take good care of and maintain our equipment. We had a homemade skate sharpener that we used to sharpen our skates. It was a hand-cranked grinder that needed to be watered manually, so it took multiple kids to sharpen a pair of skates. We took great care to preserve the equipment that we had.

My wife Linda, raised as an only child, recalls heating potatoes when she was young and stuffing them into her skate boots, leaving them in there to heat the cold, stiff leather. When she was satisfied that the boots were wearable, she would pull the spuds out and stuff her cold toes into the warm boots, nicely prepared for a trip to the frozen pond with her friends. In our family, no one would have wanted to eat boot-seasoned potatoes, and we didn't have enough to spare to warm dozens of boots and then throw those potatoes out, so we braved the cold without such luxury.

Those around me tell me that I started skating around the age of three. My parents didn't encourage us to play hockey, and while some of my family played, none of them seemed to have the passion for it that I did. I skated with a dedication and intensity that none of them matched. We skated on a dugout or slough (pronounced in Canada as *slew*), which in the warmer seasons was a pond on our property for our animals. In the cold season, I would spend six to seven hours a day on the ice if I could. For the life of me, I can't remember what I did as a young kid during the time of year when it wasn't frozen over. Maybe I was like a reverse bear who slept through the summer season. No, I guess, when the ground was warm and fertile, the summer months were reserved for farming, and I was probably so busy learning how to till, sow, and reap that I didn't have time to do much more than dream about hockey.

Many players thank their old coaches or other people that were influential in their formative years, but I cannot really think of anyone in particular that I can say had anything to do with my ability to play hockey or hone my skills other than myself and those in my immediate family. I can honestly say that I developed my skills by playing on the ponds or on the streets or playing shinny against my brothers and sisters or my friends. I never attended a hockey school; I was just told by my coaches to go out and score goals. I was not taught how to pass or shoot; I just did it naturally.

I don't remember being corrected for any plays I didn't execute properly, either. I do remember one man who came to the town of Montmartre to be our doctor and keep us well. He was Dr. Prefontaine, and he inspired the whole team because of his status, and he certainly inspired me with his play and his aggressiveness. He changed the whole hockey team and the Montmartre Hockey organization. We all benefitted from his arrival to our town and the help he gave the whole community. If I remember correctly, he had a tryout with the Quebec Aces of the American league, but I don't recall the details. I was simply a rural boy who loved to play hockey and didn't pay attention to much else.

Another influential player that came into my life and career was a gentleman named Joe Mack. Joe joined the team as a defenseman and quickly became a mentor to me. He worked for the department of highways, and I remember him pulling up to the rink after work and parking his big trailer outside. I only skated with him for a year, but he did have a tremendous influence on me, helping me with my hockey skills and helping me as a person.

Joe got me my first job outside of the home. He got me on as a roadsman for the highway department, helping build roads during my last summer home before I left to play for the Regina Pats. Joe showed me that there were good, hard-working people outside of the family and the farm. He was a very quiet person, and I had great respect for him, admiring his skills and his work ethic on and off the ice.

My siblings and I were raised on a farm during my early years and, as on all farms at the time, all the children in the household shared in the chores. While doing those chores may not have been what a child would choose given the option, I understand now that those very tasks helped build my strength and endurance through a natural conditioning process and gave me the ability to succeed in hockey as I did. I recall that I did a great deal of the wood chores—gathering, chopping, and stacking—and I credit that great workout process for the muscles that undoubtedly translated into a strong shooting arm.

On the farm, the chores we did depended on our age. The older kids were given the more difficult, complicated chores and were expected to train their replacements, patiently teaching their younger siblings how to take over their jobs. I suppose this built excitement for the younger kids, as they looked forward to the prestige of taking over the older kids' jobs. In hindsight, I don't know if that was all by clever design or happy circumstance, but either way, it worked, and we all learned and grew as a team. This setting again prepared me for life as a player on an organized sports squad.

While I don't have many specific memories of my first few years skating, I skated every day. I would do anything to skate. Sometimes I would sneak into the local covered rink at night and skate for hours alone. The sound of my skates on the ice was something that I craved, something I thought about as I ate my lunch and rushed through dinner. Somehow food just tasted better knowing that a good skate would soon follow.

In 1947, when I was about six years old, we moved from our farm into town, and all I remember about the move was that we were closer to the indoor rink. We had a dairy and delivered milk each morning until 1956. The reason we stopped in 1956 was that the government stepped in and said that the milk was not pasteurized, so we could no longer sell it. As a kid, that seemed kind of insulting, and I wondered why someone would do that to my parents. But instead of brooding about it, we moved on, and with my focus on hockey, I don't really know a lot about how family life went once I started spending a lot of time away playing hockey on other teams.

After school and on weekends, I would rush through my chores (think rapid rep's) and head to wherever the ice was. As a kid, I would clean the ice at the local rink using a hand scraper, earning usually two dollars a week from adults at the rink. The freezing wind would bite at our faces as we'd throw the shavings out the back door, but we were diligent in completing our task and pleasing the adults. The funny part of being paid two dollars is that I was actually paid with a two-dollar bill. It was fascinating to me at the time, and I didn't want to spend them. Receiving a two-dollar bill was quite special, as they were so rare and unique. Receiving payment in that way certainly helped me save, and when I eventually was able to bring myself to cash them in, there was enough to get new equipment and especially a new stick. I even still have some of those coveted two-dollar bills to this day, tucked away safely. I pull them out and look at them every now and then, and it takes me right back to my childhood.

A few of us kids also had the privilege of being the first of what would today be known as a Zamboni driver. We would fill a forty-gallon barrel on a sleigh with water from the tap out back, drag it up to the rink about a quarter of a mile, and smooth the ice with what was left in the can that wasn't frozen from the trip to the building. We would heat that hard water (you couldn't drink it) in a barrel over a fire,

4

then put it in another barrel with a valve on the back that we would pass over the ice to smooth it out. It was not quite the glamour of today's Zamboni drivers, but we were proud of our skills. It was all worth it because when the adults were done and the other kids were gone, I had the ice to myself. I'd race back and forth, back and forth, stride after stride, until it felt like my legs would buckle and my heart would pound right out of my chest. Then I'd turn off the lights, close the place up, and go home. What an honor, right? They trusted me with taking care of the place, and I learned early on that to earn someone's trust is indeed an honor, a privilege, and a responsibility not to be taken lightly—something that has served me well throughout my years.

I didn't think about it at the time, but my hours spent cleaning and grooming the ice gave me an invaluable workout and gave my game the edge that I needed to meet and beat the skills of those many years older than me. Oh, and when I was working at the rink, sometimes I got out of those darned chores at home. Kids will be kids.

I got my first new pair of skates at about the age of thirteen, a pair of skates endorsed by Maurice "Rocket" Richard that I was surprised to get at Christmas. I couldn't have been happier. They fit like no other skates had fit and served me well for a long time. I wasn't an equipment snob, and I'm still not to this day. It was definitely a tremendous advantage to have to adapt to different types of skates, sticks, and ice surfaces. Back then, our sticks were made of wood, and they were very heavy. I would tape my stick so that the tape would absorb the pass, and I used the tape to put a knob on the end to make the stick easier to hold. However, because the sticks were so heavy, I would use as little tape as possible, only taping a small portion in order to keep it as light as possible. I also used talcum powder, whereas today we use wax, but back then, I probably would have thought the wax would add too much weight, slowing down my shots and passes. But having only a small area taped meant that I had to catch passes precisely correct and always know exactly where the puck was on my stick.

True pond hockey players are skilled for all of these reasons, and no matter how much elite training I could have received, there is no way I could have been better served in my formative years than with the experience I got on and off the ice in the very setting I was in. Getting all of that training while living at home and basically "playing" with my siblings was invaluable. Coming from such a large family meant that I had a good number of teammates exhibiting various skill levels, and we all learned to teach each other and to learn from each other—all while getting along and working out any conflicts peacefully on our own. Even though hockey eventually took me away to great places and to a good life, I already had a good life and wouldn't trade my childhood for anything.

My sister Annette recalls how different things were when we were young as compared to today. We had a much harder life. When we did finally get a telephone, it was one of the old phones that you had to turn a crank on to use. Our house had no running water. If one of us drank too much water before bed and needed to go during the night, we had a "honey pot," which, for those of you who are unfamiliar, had nothing to do with actual honey, but was a pot used to urinate in so that you didn't have to make the trip to the outhouse in the freezing cold, dark night. That pot may well be the reason I shy away from the healthier version of sugar that people today put in their tea. No honey for me, thank you.

My upbringing and religion also taught me to be humble and to never be a braggart. I believe that allowed me to kind of fly under the radar at times. I was taught never to boast, that vanity was a sin, and I was never a chirper, so I didn't draw the negative attention of other players, coaches, and owners. I played on my merits, which I believe is why I was chosen by such a prominent group to be the first Winnipeg Jet, later to be tagged with the moniker The Original Jet. They saw my potential and what I could bring to the team, and it was a welcome breath of fresh air from the repression we players had experienced in the pre-WHA NHL.

I'm not sure what sparked inside of me to drive me to be so passionate about the game, much more passionate than anyone else around me. It did help that I was playing with my older siblings and being included as part of the team. I wanted to perform as well as everyone else so playing with them made me work harder to be an equal and even a superior contributor to any team I was on. When you're part of a large family, you do have to do things to stand out, and hockey must have been my way of making sure they took notice of me.

Having that built-in team meant that we didn't have to look beyond our home for friends, and I'm not sure what other kids in our area did in their pleasure time. I do know that while those kids were excited to get the Sears catalog in order to look at what was inside and dream about what they wanted for Christmas, my siblings and I grabbed those catalogs, shoved them into our boots, and gave ourselves some of the best shin guards around. Once again, I probably out-ran and out-muscled my siblings for the mail far too often. I think I better make some phone calls and let my siblings know again how much I appreciate them.

Norm's childhood home (1942)

Norm (in mother's arms) and family with their car (1942)

Norm's family

Original Zamboni

$2 Bill

Chapter Two

THIS KID JUST WANTS TO PLAY HOCKEY

Anyone who knows me knows that people are important to me, and of course, the first people in my world were my parents and my immediate family. My parents were both French Canadians, and we grew up speaking French. It's amazing to me to think that here we are, well into the 2000s, and my father Martial was born in the 1800s—1896 to be precise. My mother, Fernande, was born in 1909, and they married when she was twenty years old and he was thirty-three. My mom gave birth to thirteen children over the span of twenty years. Of the thirteen children my mother gave birth to, all of us were born at home except for the last one, who was born in the hospital and unfortunately passed away. Back in those days, people didn't talk much about things like that so I'm not sure what happened, but that was the last baby born to my parents, as my father passed away on May 21st of 1970.

My father was the nicest guy I have ever met. He was so kindhearted, and he had the demeanor of a true gentleman. I learned more from him than anyone else. He treated people well, which I believe is the greatest lesson I have ever learned. He didn't complain; he just worked, provided for us, and showed us an example of how to be a good person. I always wanted to be just like him when I grew up, with one exception: fewer children.

My mother was no different. All she did was work. Non-stop, from the time her feet hit the floor until she put them back in bed at night. She and my sisters deserve medals for how hard they worked to make a good home for our family. As a family, we never went on vacation. There was always work to do, and any spare time that we had was spent with extended family and helping out the community as we were best able.

In the home, we spoke only French, which was the only language I knew when I started school. School was taught in English with one hour of French class, and although I could somewhat read French, writing it? Not so much. I still speak French fluently, and some other languages, but the writing doesn't come easily to me. Before I began attending school, I had only really interacted with family members, as our farm was near an Indian reservation and our only other neighbors were our French cousins, so there wasn't a need to speak a language other than French until I started school. As one can imagine, learning English became a priority as soon as I walked in the doors of school that first day. I don't recall my older siblings mentioning this challenge; it was just a fact of life. It seems we each faced the obstacle and overcame it without complaint.

Life was simple on the farm and free from the pressures of materialism, frivolities, and negative outside influences. We occasionally listened to radio shows, as we didn't have television, and even the people in town who did have TV didn't have very good pictures. When I was a bit older, I did go into town to watch the TV at Tom Percival's auto shop, as he had one of the only TVs in town. It was the biggest TV any of us had seen, and we could see it through his window from the outside. On Friday nights, I would go to a friend's house to watch "Gunsmoke." So, that was the sum total of our television entertainment back then. Entertainment was found at home in the company of each other, which was fine with me. I didn't even leave home until I was fifteen, which was to play junior hockey. I am thankful for my stable childhood and look back fondly on all the memories I carry with me.

As I mentioned, one of the big advantages of having so many siblings was that I had a built-in hockey team. Even my five sisters played at times, but we only played after the chores were done. We had a pretty big farm: 300 acres of pasture and 450 acres of cultivated land. We had cattle, chickens, horses, and pigs. It takes a lot of hands to care for all that land and to feed and care for all of those animals. Together, we all worked hard to get everything done before we hit the ice.

I think it is important to acknowledge all of the children in my family. In birth order, they are:

Name	Occupation
Alain, deceased	Farmer
Harvey, deceased	Farmer
Lorraine, deceased	Clerk
Edwin	Construction
Annette	Several jobs

Claude, deceased	Builder, truck driver
Leona	Secretary, housewife
France	Secretary, housewife
Norm (myself)	
Jocelyn	Secretary, housewife, interpreter
Aurel	Hockey player, miner, coach
Bob	Construction
Florence, deceased	Passed away as an infant

As my siblings and I are reaching our older years, several have passed, and that always brings about sobering thoughts. Also, still very sad are my memories of the passing of my youngest sister Florence, who died at birth. All of us were born at home with the exception of Florence, who was born at the hospital so I suspect they did know that something was wrong but we children were not included in those discussions. I do recall the funeral for her. Watching my father carry the tiny, wooden casket is forever etched into my brain and onto my heart. I recall vividly the pattern of the wood, the long dresses on the women, and the long faces on everyone there. I hadn't been to many funerals up to that time and certainly not to one for a sibling. Even with many shoulders to lean on, those shoulders shook with grief, and that was a very difficult time for every one of us.

One of the downsides to having all those children is that there weren't places to put them all. After a great day on the ice we went home to fall asleep in shared beds. There was no thought of having our own bed, much less our own bedroom. One would think then that being in a billeted home later and having my own bed would have felt really good, but it was lonely. Maybe that was a good thing because it just made me throw myself harder into the game, to escape the thoughts that plague athletes when they are out of their element. I was always very happy to see everyone when I was home.

Meals at home were simple but good. We had meat from our animals, often beef, pork roast, or chicken for dinner, along with potatoes and whatever vegetable was available. I can only imagine how many chickens my mother and sisters had to cook to feed all of us. Mealtime was important; we appreciated the food that was on our table and said grace before every meal. Although we shared beds, we each had our own place at the giant dining table that would seat fourteen people and expanded for guests.

I also recall my father saying "Cheers" or "Santé" to toast. To me it was an important acknowledgement of the food and drink we had in front of us, and I still, to this day, like to make a salutation before having a drink with friends. It is a way to show gracious appreciation for the sustenance before us, and I have learned this in many languages throughout my travels. I have included a list of these salutations at the end of this book.

We had family traditions that I remember fondly. We had an indoor tree, and we went to midnight Mass on Christmas Eve. We would find our socks stuffed with small gifts. I can recall one year getting a new hockey stick and another year getting the Rocket Richard skates. Wow, that was a great Christmas! I recall one Christmas when we boys were a bit late arriving to church, so we tried to sneak in unnoticed. We quietly climbed the stairs and made it to the loft without much ado until my brother Harvey sat down and slid over to his spot, promptly letting out a blood-curdling scream. Suddenly, all eyes were upon us, and we were busted. As Harvey had slid down the wooden bench, he neglected to see a large sliver of wood sticking up, and as he made his way to his spot, the bench gifted him with a three-inch sliver embedded deep into his backside. It took quite some time and effort to remove that memento, as I recall. Just punishment for being late, we all figured.

I was a good kid for the most part, but I was a kid at the same time. The one holiday a year when we would go a little crazy was Halloween. Candy and apples were not enough to appease our appetite for adventure and when we would go out trick or treating, as most groups of young guys will do, we would play stupid games, trying to out-do each other. I don't know what it was, but Halloween, in particular, brought out the little prankster in me. We would tip over outhouses, topple cords of wood, do just about whatever we could to shake things up without doing too much damage.

One Halloween, one of my teachers was ready for us. We tipped over the outdoor toilet and BAM! There he was. He looked at us and bellowed, "Gentlemen of the manure pile" and proceeded to chastise us. As he spoke, I realized how stupid I had behaved. I was so embarrassed and ashamed. The next day in class was torturous. I still feel guilty to this day about the stupid little pranks we pulled on All Hallow's Eve. After that, I pretty much stuck to safer things, like hockey.

One thing I did enjoy doing that was not competitive was horseback riding. We rode horses on the farm for herding cattle and used them for other chores. My favorite horse was Pearl. She was a fast, light brown horse that we used on the farm to deliver milk and pull the sleigh. I fed her hay, oats, and sugar cubes. She would lap them up with gentle lips as I pet her soft, furry muzzle. I always rode bareback, and Pearl just seemed to know me and what I needed.

One day when I was maybe seven or eight years old, my father said no riding. Well, I didn't see the reasoning in that and my buddy (also named Norm) and I took off for a ride. I was galloping downhill on one of the older, bigger horses, and she, the not-so-agile thing that she was, tumbled and flipped over on me. Let me tell you, I was hurt. The horse got right up, but me? Not so quickly. I was knocked out for a while. I had a deep gash on my chin, and I knew I was in trouble. Once again, I should have stuck with something less dangerous, like hockey.

Other than Pearl, I never got really close with the farm animals. I liked them—I like animals in general and they seem to like me—but I didn't tend to get too close to them. I remember around 1957, during one particularly violent electrical storm, a few of us kids were looking outside, watching the lightning when a strike tore down. There was a huge flash in the field. Instantly, we realized that lightning had hit Tessy, Pearl's mother, and she went down quicker than the mare that had tumbled on me. I suppose watching that affected me a bit and kept me from getting too close to the animals after that. Perhaps Tessy should have tried hockey.

Oftentimes my siblings were too busy or couldn't it make it to my games, so they didn't see many of them. My father didn't watch me play hockey. He was too busy working and taking care of the family farm, but I never resented him for that. Some kids had parents there watching them play, but I felt like my dad had important things to do and that I was doing my job, working hard to stand out as an exceptional hockey player. It's not that he wasn't interested in my playing, but he did not go overboard as far as getting involved—probably to avoid showing preference for one child over the others. My mother was more into hockey, not just because of me but because she liked the game. Sadly, she didn't get to see me play at a high level. God bless her soul; she deserved more.

While playing with my family was handy and enjoyable, I expanded my opportunities as soon as I was able. I played for every organized group I could, playing in school and with higher-tier organizations, which included playing with adults at a very young age. I wasn't intimidated because my oldest brother was eleven years older than me, and I was accustomed to matching up against much older and larger individuals than me. Speed and agility were the edges I had against bigger players.

In school, while it's not a term that I'm really comfortable applying to myself, I was called "the hometown star." I started with the Montmartre Canadiens when I was fourteen. We made the playoffs, and I played on the All-Star team. I loved that I got to play with my older brothers. After the games, when everyone would go out to rehash the game over brews, my brothers would be there to watch over me and make sure I conducted myself as a proper young man. Because that was such a great way to grow up, as I have lived through the years, I have strived to be that guiding light for others, both on and off the ice. I try to be there for people, especially those who don't have the family that I have.

My sister Lorraine was always there for others, as well. When I was playing as a teen, I recall so many times how Lorraine would cook meals for me and my teammates. Huge, delicious meals to be devoured by ravenous players with huge appetites. Even if she didn't make it to the game, she was there afterward to make sure we had what we needed.

While my family wasn't able to watch all of my games, senior hockey was aired on the radio, and they got to listen when I was in Saskatchewan for the adult play-offs. Even though I couldn't see them, it always felt good knowing that they could hear what was going on. Unlike many families today, I could always rely on the stability of my parents as a couple and united voice, as well as my siblings and my extended family. While I grew up with the pressures of having to work so very hard, I think many people today face tougher challenges than I did, with divided families, a lack of loyalty, impatience with others, and the ever-present social media. I am abundantly grateful for the setting in which I was raised.

Another stable factor throughout my life has been my religion. I was raised Catholic. My family was Catholic, obviously. I had twelve brothers and sisters, I guess that's really Catholic! I was an altar boy for almost five years in my hometown of Montmartre. When Linda and I got married, she became Catholic, and we raised our children Catholic. They all made First Communion and Confirmation while we were in Switzerland. I never deviated from my religion no matter the circumstances—and life has thrown quite the circumstances at me from time to time.

When I played hockey, I tried to attend mass every Sunday wherever we played. Sometimes it was impossible to attend, but I tried to make the best of it every week, even while I was on the road. I also tried to say my rosary as much as possible—so again, I never deviated from my religion, no matter if things were good or bad.

As a family, my dad rented a pew each year, so we did go to mass at different times. Some of us were altar boys, and our large group attended mass every Sunday and also Holy Days of Obligation. My dad said his prayers every night, kneeling down, or we said it as a family. I didn't see weakness in his kneeling; I saw wisdom and strength that he would speak to the Creator. I am so thankful to have had that background and foundation set out before me.

I'm not pushing my religion on anyone. I never have. I'm not one to preach, but if someone asks, I will happily share. Thus, it's part of this book, as it is a part of me— an important part. I'll share my story, and in the end, to each his own. In my own experience, when I put God first, everything else falls into line. And while I stand behind the doctrine of "to each his own," I will say that I have seen those who put themselves or other individuals before God and it never seems to work out for them in the end. That's not to say that I haven't seen religious individuals sin or make mistakes, but they seem to be the first to recognize the magnitude of their wrongdoing and seek redemption in an effort to make things right. It always feels good knowing you and those around you are playing by the same set of rules. That's not to say that everything has always gone smoothly for me. Even though I was working my way to fulfilling my dreams, there were times that got me down.

One of the worst memories I have of my younger years is from a playoff hockey game when I was fourteen while playing for Montmartre. The other team from Fairlight, Saskatchewan had a monster of a guy—maybe only fourteen years old but about 6'2" and a great player. To cut it short, they beat us, beat us bad. That kid dominated the playoffs, and I was devastated. I cried and couldn't even eat the next day. It still takes a while for me to recover mentally from a loss, but that one was the worst.

When I think about it, life is like a game. You don't know going in if it will be a long season, if you will make it to the playoffs, if you'll be hurt, or if you'll take The Cup. However, I think if you lie on your death bed knowing you did well by your fellow teammates, put in your best effort, and stayed true to your morals, then you've won anyway.

Having that inner focus and stability readied me for situations, both off and on the ice. Living by a credo and with stable morals allows one to focus on other things rather than contemplating one's actions in various situations. My religious beliefs have allowed me to walk through life with a confidence that comes from knowing that I'm following the rules and doing what I am supposed to do, if that makes sense. Not only has my faith kept me humble, which I believe is important in an athlete and competitor, it carried me through the very difficult times that were to come.

Norm (front), his siblings, and Uncle Emile (~1945)

Chapter Three

THIS BIG KID JUST WANTS TO PLAY HOCKEY

Being a hockey player in a small town in Canada was no special thing. The thought of going big-time as a professional player seemed unachievable to many, but for me, it just seemed as though it was written in the stars. I knew if I did my job (play, train, play, train, and play some more), I would just keep on moving up. It was a foregone conclusion in my mind, and I have no idea why.

I didn't come from a strong hockey pedigree. Sure, my father and brothers (and sisters) played, but I didn't want to just *play*, I wanted to *get paid to play*. As I was growing up, because ice was not readily available in the warmer months, I turned to releasing my energy through playing pretty much any physical sport I could. I recall playing soccer in the snow when I was a kid. But we had to play with a brown ball because who can see a white ball in the snow and white-out conditions?

I also played football. I was the quarterback for the high school football team. The ball was already brown, so that wasn't anything special, but I did do pretty well for the team. High school sports were a big deal back then, just as they are today, and I was happy to represent my town. I also played baseball and participated in curling.

Nevertheless, I was happiest when I was representing a hockey team—usually, that is. One year when I was fourteen or fifteen, I was playing senior hockey with the adults in a New Year's Day game. The adults were still hungover or maybe still inebriated because it wasn't the greatest game, but it was a game I wanted to *win*. The game was tied one to one going into the final minutes, and because everyone (except for me, I guess) was so tired, one of the opposing players flung a puck from the far end of the ice toward our goalie. Well, our goalie wasn't ready for that, and I swear I could have read the label as the puck slid ever so slowly down the ice, coast to coast, and went right under the goalie's stick into the net. It was one of the first games I played looking up to adults, and they really let me down. We lost two to one, and I hoped their hangovers would stick with them for weeks. They did have some good players on that other team from Estevan, Saskatchewan. One of them, Ernie "Punch" McLean, went on to become the owner of a junior team and has accumulated quite the array of awards over the years.

One highlight that offset some of the losses was when I was presented a watch by none other than Brenda Lee. There was a ceremony at Eaton's Department store and awards were being presented for player of the year and rookie of the year. She was younger than me, but she was a star. And I was starstruck—starstruck to the point where I could feel my cheeks getting hot, and the only reason they didn't glow red in the newspaper article photograph is because they only printed in black and white, thankfully. I felt like the luckiest guy on the planet.

I was also one of the lucky kids who didn't get physically hurt too badly during my young years. The most serious injury that I recall was one time when I was fourteen playing senior hockey and got hit by a pretty big defenseman who literally knocked me out. I did bounce back quickly, but in today's world, I probably would have been benched for a while.

Like I mentioned before, I did not have the luxury of having coaches that really helped me. I must say that these days, in hockey, and really all sports, kids have so many advantages compared to what we had. They have opportunities to improve their skills with good coaching, good equipment, great facilities, better diets, training camps, private lessons, access to information online—you name it, they can get it. Great coaching is key, and with all the chances kids have to improve their skills, if they have the passion, they can excel at not just hockey but any sport they desire to play. They also have the ability and opportunity to pursue an education through hockey scholarships, which one of my sons took advantage of.

From my experience, very few professional hockey players have drug problems or the scope of problems off the ice that we see in other professional sports. I attribute that in part to what ends up being a sort of screening process. The parents put in a great deal of time, money, and effort to get their kids to a high level of hockey, so the family effort and the sacrifices show. Additionally, when the kids go to play on other teams and are billeted with other families, they learn to be respectful and integrate into that family, contributing and earning their way, because if they don't, and the billeted team lets them go, there are a great many players ready to take their place. Therefore, the athletes must earn their way on and off the ice, sometimes from quite a young age, meeting and surmounting multiple challenges along the way.

Even as a young, natural athlete, I was faced with personal challenges. While injuries as a kid were kept to a minimum, when I was first playing for the Regina

Pats at the age of sixteen, the coach told me one day that I needed to get my eyes checked. I thought he was crazy, but I did as he said and went to see a specialist. I was blindsided by the news that I was, in fact, legally blind in my right eye. The doctor diagnosed me with keratoconus, which is a cone-shaped cornea. Turns out the thing is so cone shaped that I couldn't see a puck flying at me from the right. Perhaps that's why I often didn't seem to be afraid of getting hit by one, not even flinching when it was whizzing in my direction from that side. It was a condition that I must have had from birth. Maybe it was so cold that night I was born that my eyeball froze.

I've learned that people who are blind have better hearing, so perhaps the malformed cornea was actually an advantage for me, sharpening another vital sense to the point of my having superior hearing and a distinct advantage over others once I was able to see properly—or not, but I'll go with that. That's my superpower.

So, immediately after that first eye-doctor visit, I was fitted with a contact and what a difference it made! Being one-eye blind since birth, I hadn't known any better, but wow, when I could see clearly with both eyes, the concentration that I had put into watching everything with that one eye was doubled, and I took off! That is, when I had that contact over my conic cornea. While I only needed one contact, at the time, contacts were prescribed in pairs, so I always had a spare, which turned out to be a good thing. Lenses back then were made of a hard, uncomfortable material and every now and then, that sucker would just go rogue and pop right out. More than once, a game or practice was stopped so our team could look for my renegade contact. One time, we found it right in front of the net. Another time, the glint showed from on top of the blue line. I recall losing one on the bench, later finding it stuck between the wood slats. Miraculously, they almost always turned up undamaged. Almost.

Kismet. Call it kismet, destiny, fate, or whatever, but when I was about seventeen or eighteen years old playing for the Regina Pats of the Saskatchewan Junior Hockey League, something in me flinched, and I accidentally hit a puck into the stands. I watched in horror as the puck hit this cute girl. While she wasn't hurt, I'm sure she wasn't amused. My billet partner saw what had happened and told me he knew the girl. He said he would introduce me to her so that I could apologize. After the game, my friend introduced me to the girl named Linda, and I was smitten—to use an era-appropriate term.

As a young player, I was still busy playing and traveling, but Linda and I saw each other whenever we could. We had a lot of fun together. She called me her "partner in crime" and fit right in with my hockey family. I was her first experience with the hockey world. She was a figure skater whose exposure to a frozen sheet of ice usually consisted of the one at the community center. I was always surprised when I saw her, the usually quiet, polite, well-mannered, tiny, young lady, sitting in the stands, mittened fists clenched into tense, angry balls, yelling at my opponents.

On New Year's Eve of 1962, we were sitting at a table with a group of my friends. The table was buzzing with excitement and everyone else was speaking French, so Linda couldn't understand a word of what they were saying. Nevertheless, I worked up the courage to ask her to marry me that night, and luckily, she accepted. She rode the train home that night and later told me that she was sitting in her seat when the conductor came by with the ring she had left in the bathroom. That wasn't the only hurdle we faced in getting our relationship off the ground. When Linda returned home and showed her mother the engagement ring I had given her, her mother said simply, "Give it back." Perhaps she knew of the darker side of the hockey world and the hardships we would certainly face. Good thing for me, Linda was a bit rebellious and didn't follow her mom's advice. We were married the following year, in 1963 in Regina, Saskatchewan at St. Mary's Church with about 250 people in attendance.

Sometime after the wedding, I was told that when one of Linda's bridesmaids walked into the reception, she brought a new date with her. Not knowing much about him, Linda and her friend were quite surprised when the couple walked in and a bunch of my groomsmen ran over to the guy, ready to throw him out. It turned out that he was a player on a rival team, and my teammates did as they would on the ice: they had my back. Fortunately for all, Linda and her friend were able to calmly explain what was going on before anyone got hurt (that the new guy was not crashing our wedding). Although I think Linda's friend had a bit of explaining to do to him later, given that she had walked him right into the lion's den. He must not have been too upset with her though, as they were later married and remain so to this day.

Not all flying pucks were quite as lucky for me as the one that brought Linda and me together. I got injured again in 1959 when someone shot the puck right at my face and knocked me out. I made the trip to the hospital to get twenty stitches on my cheek bone, but I managed to heal quickly and played several days later. I didn't want to miss any hockey that year or any year.

As I replay these moments in my head, I am reminded that I made it through a variety of my own injuries, even though when we started writing this book, I felt like I hadn't been injured much. I recall, during my time with the Pats, getting hit in the mouth by a stick and needing to see the dentist. Being from a rural farming family of limited means, we didn't see the dentist regularly like people do today. We only went when we had a toothache so severe that home remedies or pliers couldn't fix it. So, this dentist thing was new. I quickly learned that I actually *liked* it. The dentist had this amazing ability to make the pain go away. I would go there with a new injury, and even some lingering old ones, and I would leave feeling like a new man. I got to really like the dentist and was quite happy to return whenever I needed to. Some people don't like the sound of the drill, but it's the happy sound of relief to me.

As a side note, something I always tell my students is to wear something to cover their faces—a shield or cage, something to protect the moneymaker—because even though they *think* they may be quick enough to dodge a puck, they won't always see the stick coming. Even if they do see it coming, they may not be able to get out of the way before it sends them to the dentist—or, even worse, the facial surgeon. So, equipment up, kids. It's available for a reason.

Although violence wasn't a big part of my game, that's not to say I didn't put the hurt on opposing players if I needed to. You couldn't survive in that league without letting the other players know you meant business. Sometimes, though, in hockey, things just happen. Such as in one game I was playing in for the Pats. We were playing against the Moosejaw Canucks, and I got a breakaway. I tore up the ice, faked a shot, pulled back my stick, zagged, and backhanded a shot right at the net. Damn if that goalie didn't anticipate my zag, and my stick whacked him right in the eye. To top it off, that goalie was none other than Joe Lech—the guy that had almost been thrown out of my wedding reception. I felt terrible. He left the game, and they put another goalie in. I scored two goals after that, before learning that Joe was going to need to have his head immobilized in a halo to try to heal his eye.

Joe and I weren't friends at the time of his injury, but I got to know him later, as we become reacquainted. He and his wife Sue recently visited us in Arizona after celebrating their fiftieth wedding anniversary. We had a great time reliving the past, even though I was responsible for sending his career on a different path. It turns out that with that injury, a professional career became out of the question. However, there were silver linings, and Joe got a full scholarship to college. He played for the North Dakota Gophers and earned his college degree. So now he says that I am *responsible* for him getting his degree—or that I am *to blame* for him getting his degree, depending on his mood.

Since we were married, Linda has gone everywhere with me. Hockey players move time after time, after time, from the beginning of training camp or training camps, to regular season, perhaps being traded up and down in the leagues during the season, and then back home again after the season is over. We have moved countless times across towns, states, provinces, countries, continents, and seas. Some wives choose to stay put in a single location while their hockey-playing husbands travel from town to town and team to team, but Linda was different, always there by my side.

The early years didn't make us financially rich, but they were rich in experience. If you must move, embrace it. Get to know new people, new foods, new environments, new cultures. The United States, even though it is fairly young by most standards, is rich in heritage and opportunity for growth. Linda and I consider ourselves very fortunate to be blessed with the opportunity to live there. Throughout my career, moving many times allowed us to immerse ourselves in many different cultures.

1962/63 Hull Ottawa Canadiens

In 1962, I went to the Montreal training camp to try to make the Montreal Canadiens hockey team. After about a month of training camp, I made the team. When it was time to start negotiating my contract, I had to meet with a couple of men by the names of Scotty Bowman and Sam Pollock. They asked me what I wanted to play for, and I told them I wanted a $1000 signing bonus and $5000 to play. There I was, a nineteen-year-old kid from Regina, Saskatchewan, who had just finished a pretty illustrious three-year career with the Regina Pats. Everyone knew that I never had any problems when I played for the Regina Pats; I never gave the organization any trouble; and I conducted myself with good character, on and off the ice. I thought that I did my share in helping out what was the oldest and probably the top junior franchise in history. I thought that should (and would) be recognized and valued. I had no professional guidance or experience in negotiating contracts, but I was a reasonable young man.

It quickly became apparent that I was way off base. They took the stance that I should feel lucky to even be talking to the organization. So, when I made my request, Scotty Bowman went nuts. Sam Pollock was there listening to what I proposed but Scotty had the last word, and boy was he pissed—so pissed that he jumped on the coffee table and he screamed, "Who do you think you are, coming from Saskatchewan?" and continued saying that he would send me, "So far north that '*Hockey News*' will never find you." I heard that I was not the only one to have that line thrown at him, but even knowing I was in good company, it hurt.

Little did I know that Sam would become the manager of the Canadiens, and Scotty would be the winningest coach in the NHL—but that's really irrelevant. For some reason, from that first meeting, Scotty Bowman took a disliking to me and wherever we went, he made life difficult for me. I never could figure it out or make things better. He was just determined to have a bad relationship with me. Had I toppled his woodpile and dumped over his outhouse back in the day?

Anyway, I did sign the measly contract that they put in front of me, and I went to play for the Hull Ottawa Canadiens. I did have a pretty good year playing with guys like Terry Harper, Claude Larose, Jacques LaPerriere, Cesare Maniago, and Red Barenson. I was playing with top guys that eventually played with the Montreal Canadiens and had pretty good careers.

With Bowman, I was competing on and off the ice. With him, I lost. The way they did it, if they could save some money for the organization somehow, they would do it. They'd put money in their own pocket, undoubtedly. If they could cut everybody's pay by a couple grand, it was a feather in their caps for the organization, in the eyes of the owners, and in their own pockets, of course.

We players were left holding the bag, and the reason you would agree to a contract like that is because you knew that you had no say, no power. They controlled you; they owned you; and they could do whatever they wanted with you—and they did. They treated us like mere commodities, like lowly animals.

That year, I blew out my knee, and I was put in a cast because of stretched ligaments. I had the cast on for a week, and Scotty Bowman asked me if I could play. I dared not say no, so I removed my cast and played that same night. No therapy, nothing. Hockey *was* my therapy. At that time, I figured I had an NHL career in the future that would eventually support my family, but not at that point, especially if I didn't play. Back then, the league, the owners, and the managers didn't care if playing injured would ruin a player's health or career; they just wanted to win the next game at any cost. So, injured or not, I played.

Aside from the struggles, one of the great things about playing professionally was the equipment that we got. We were brought directly to the factories—Louisville, Sherwood, etc.—to choose our favorite sticks, have them sized, and get all outfitted with the best. That was nice. That way, if we were in a town with a big factory, we would use their equipment, and make them proud of their products.

Recently, as I was watching a game between the Carolina Hurricanes and Toronto Maple Leafs, the EBUG (emergency backup goalie) David Ayres (an AHL Zamboni driver) was called up, stopped eight of the ten shots on him, and brought home the W for the 'Canes. Seeing the buzz about the event reminded me of the time I pulled off a unique feat, scoring as a forward and playing goalie. I don't know if I'm the only player to score and also play goalie in the same game, but it was quite the to-do!

1963/64 Red Wings, Pittsburgh Hornets, Indianapolis Capitols, Cincinnati Wings
After my first year playing professionally with the Hull Ottawa Canadiens, I was drafted by the Detroit Red Wings. I went to training camp with the Red Wings in 1963 for the 63/64 season. Training camp went well. The organization seemed to have much of the same attitude as I had experienced prior, but it was a little better to deal with. They treated their players a bit better than Montreal because, as I mentioned earlier, the Montreal organization tended to have the take that if you were in their organization, they were paying you homage by simply allowing you to belong to the Montreal Canadiens. Thus, they had the attitude that *you* owed *them*, and that was wrong. Plain and simple, it was wrong. It was the wrong attitude and the wrong

way to treat people, but we had no choice at the time. We had no union, no leaders, no organized way to address the unfair practices that we were subjected to.

I went to the Detroit Red Wings training camp right after Linda and I were married in August. After training camp, there I was, again, at the negotiating table, this time with Jack Adams and, I think, maybe Sid Abel. Jack Adams did most of the talking, and I went through the same thing there that I had with Scotty Bowman. I had been drafted by the Red Wings, and I thought I had a pretty good chance of making the team with the likes of Gordie Howe, Alex Delveccio, Terry Sawchuck, and Paul Henderson, who was my age.

I recall that Paul Henderson was instrumental in scoring that big goal in September against the Russians in the dying minutes of the 1972 Summit Series hockey game. So again, there I was, involved with guys of this caliber: Gordie Howe, future hall-of-famers. It was an honor to be at the Red Wings training camp, so I went in and tried to negotiate my contract but ended up with the same problem as I did with Jack Adams—the typical stance that they would cut players' pay as much as possible and be damned how it affected those players and their families. Same thing, different team. There I was looking at making a good hockey career for myself, looking at playing in the NHL with the Red Wings, so, as discouraged as I was, I signed the contract they offered me. Playing hockey in those days, even at that level, was far from as glamorous as most people thought.

From there, the Wings sent me to Indianapolis, and Linda came with me. We had our team all set up, and we were thinking that we had a pretty good hockey team. Then disaster struck. We were facing another one of life's challenges, although the challenge for me was nothing compared to the challenges and devastation that was inflicted on many others on Halloween night, 1963.

We were not playing hockey, but the place was packed with over 4,000 attendees, watching a Holiday on Ice performance when an explosion in the lower area leveled the arena—absolutely decimated the place. More than 400 people were injured, and seventy-four people were killed. The worst of it happened right in the area where the players' families would have been sitting in, and I thank God that we were not playing and that my family was not among the crowd that night. The explosion was later attributed to a propane leak.

Once the smoke cleared, literally, it was realized that we were left with no arena in which to play, so, here we go again on the move. We had been on the road at the time of the explosion, and our parent organization, the Red Wings, decided to just let us stay on the road. The building was not safe to play in, and it would take months for repairs to be completed. Therefore, the Red Wings worked out a deal to move us to Cincinnati, creating the Cincinnati Wings. In the meantime, we had no home to play in, so all our games were on the road. Quite the challenge.

That season didn't go great for me, as we were constantly on the road and everything in my life seemed to be breaking down. To add insult to injury, the tendon in my right thumb was broken. The Detroit Red Wings told me I had to go to Detroit for medical attention. The doctors there put a cast on me, and I played with that cast on for about six weeks until it was repaired. That was a very trying time in my life, playing with a cast, but I didn't want to take any more time off than I had to because if you don't have a good season then your negotiating status falls apart. If you haven't played or if you haven't played *well*, it all matters, so I just continued to play as well as I could with the cast on, pushing through the pain.

We also had a significant personal challenge arise during that time when Linda suffered a miscarriage. As a new wife, watching all the other players and their wives growing their families, Linda wanted a child very badly. Becoming a part of my big family full of loving siblings made her yearn to create the same for us, and she was devastated when she lost our first baby. But good things would come in time, both on and off the ice; some things were under our direction, and other things were out of our control.

Coaches can also control and manipulate how things appear in many ways, and they can make a player look good or make a player look bad. If you're on a good line, you can score and that looks good. If you're the better guy on the line, you can score more if the other linemen can get the puck to you. Coaches can set up helicopter lines and donut lines. These would be front lines with no wings and no centers, respectively. Even if it might make you look better than the wings, you won't look too good if you're the center on a helicopter line. Therefore, you want to stay on the right side of the coaching staff.

Regardless of how we stood with the staff, after the arena tragedy, we were left with no reasonable assistance from the organization—no help for us having to travel extensively, no help for the wives. We had to find our way to a different city, find new housing, and move all on our own. Much of those tasks were left to the wives, as we were on the road in the bus we called The Iron Lung. We crisscrossed back and forth and went all over the place for about two months with no home base. We eventually started playing our games in Cincinnati after they got all the contracts finalized with the arena, but it was a pretty dismal time for the players and our families.

With all of the problems that were no fault of ours, we took the brunt of the problems financially and mentally. It was a very difficult situation, living in the bus with no per diem compensation. We just had to live with it, again, thinking that we were lucky to have a chance to play in the big league. We just rolled with the punches.

One way to deal with the situation was to blow off steam playing pranks on each other. An occasionally vicious one was played on the first teammate to fall asleep. We would put a pack of matches on the sole of his shoe or boot and light it up. It would take a minute to take effect but talk about a rude awakening. Way to encourage guys to stay awake and engage his fellow teammates, right? Give him the "hot foot" treatment.

We had a lot of fun in airports and hotels. We would tie a fine string onto a five-dollar bill, put it on the ground, and yank the string when someone went to pick it up. A juvenile prank but funny every time. Another especially humiliating prank was when one of our teammates would leave his bag unattended. Just like in airports today, do not leave your bags unattended or you may come back from the restroom and find all the suitcase contents strewn about on chairs, rails, escalators—you name it. You always knew to travel with good underwear because you wouldn't want your church undies (the holey ones) strolling along the people-mover for the whole world to see. Despite these childish antics, some of us still made the leap to the big-league.

There were several players who eventually made it to the NHL; at the time, we were also playing with Doug Messier—Mark Messier's dad, who was there—and with him we just tried to make the best of it. I played until about March in Cincinnati, and then I was sent to the Pittsburgh Hornets of the American Hockey League. I had to leave my wife all alone in Cincinnati with no one to help her, and the team's leadership and the league just didn't care. The players were objects that they could put on the ice and exploit, making some money and developing players to do the same thing all over again. That's what we were up against all the time, young kids really, finding our own way as much as possible with no help or guidance and no compensation for travel or relocation. The tension of having to fight to hold our heads above water financially put strains on the relationships between players and managers, as well, which undoubtedly affected gameplay, even though we didn't want it to.

Through the difficult times, we found opportunities to get together with family and friends to make light of the situations we were in. Linda recounts a time she was alone in Cincinnati and I had just been sent to play in Pittsburgh. Two of my brothers and two of their friends had jobs driving cars for a dealership from Kansas City to Toronto. They stopped in Cincinnati and picked up Linda. She had been packing to move with me to Pittsburgh for the last month or so of the season, so they loaded her and as much of our belongings as they could fit in their cars, leaving space for a cooler full of beer. Linda was dressed in full fashion as always and made the trek to Pittsburgh with those boys. When they arrived, they got one hotel room, filled the cooler with what they said was dinner, along with some more beer, and the five of them headed to the arena to watch my game.

As the game began, one of the guys asked the others if they wanted a hot dog. That sounded appealing to all, even Linda, who was quite hungry by that time. Until the guy opened the cooler and passed down a single wiener, no bun—just handed a wiener down the line with his bare hand. Linda said everyone in the crowd around them looked at them like they were hillbillies, but it didn't stop the boys from enjoying their dinner. After the game, we went to the hotel, and all six of us slept in one room. Ah, the glamorous life of a professional hockey player.

As we did every year, when the hockey season concluded, we went on the road again, going back home to the snow and the cold. We went home to work so we could make enough money to survive because our paycheck from hockey just didn't cut it for the whole year. As we reminisce, Linda and I agree that Pittsburgh was one of our favorite cities. The people were great, although the weather and snow were lousy. It seemed like it snowed every day. We lived up in the Allegheny Mountains and there was soot from the factories, but overall, Pittsburgh was very nice. Nevertheless, when my hockey season ended, I had to go home to look for a job for the summer. That specific time, our life together was about to change drastically. Linda was pregnant with our son Dave. We went back to Regina and lived there for the summer until training camp came in September.

While we were in Regina that summer, I, not one to stay idle, played on a baseball team. One weekend we were at a tournament, and Linda, being pregnant, had to use the facilities. Those facilities consisted of a single portable toilet—the kind no one chooses to use unless it's an emergency. The toilet was strategically placed as far away from the playing field as it could be so that the associated odor wouldn't interfere with our enjoyment of the game. Well, Linda felt like her case was an emergency, so she entered the tiny room. She must have closed the door a little too hard and the handle on the outside slid down, locking her in. She spent the entire game in that dreadful little room until someone found her locked inside. I'm not sure she's attended a game since. Maybe that's why she doesn't complain about me playing hockey.

1964/65 Memphis Red Wings

That brings us to September of 1964. I went to the Red Wings training camp again and like a broken record, we had the same problem with the contract. Management would say what they wanted to pay me and seemed to have no recollection of the challenges we had faced and played through *for them* during the previous season. What had happened had been due to no fault of ours, but management took the position that it wasn't their problem. They didn't worry about or care about the families; players just had to adhere to what management wanted. Of course with no hockey association at that time, we had no leverage at all to help our situation. Nobody was there to say, "here, we'll get you this" or "we'll get you that," so I was on my own. It was very difficult to negotiate or fight for myself, and now suddenly, I had a family, so I couldn't just quit and walk away. I had far too much invested. Therefore, I sucked up any feelings of discontent and discouragement and put them away to deal with later, which I guess I am doing here, hoping that kids today will realize how fortunate they are and learn how to treat people right when they are in a position of authority.

After the 64/65 season training camp, I was assigned to Memphis, Tennessee: the home of Elvis Presley. Hockey was introduced to Memphis in October of 1964, and we were called the Memphis Wings: a club affiliated with the Red Wings, of course. We had guys like Glen Sather on our team, and he ended up being one of the top guys in the WHA with the Edmonton Oilers in 1973. He went on to become the coach of the Oilers in the NHL, and they won, I think, four Stanley Cups with Gretzky.

In addition to playing with stars on the rink, my position in the sports world would put us next to prominent figures in the entertainment industry as well. In Detroit in 1964, I met Danny Thomas at a Catholic church I attended. The church was packed, but I was fortunate to meet him afterward. He didn't seem to be a hockey fan. Years later, I think in 1970 or so, I also met his daughter, Marlo Thomas. We met in Cleveland, Ohio when I was working the phones, taking pledges for a telethon for St. Jude Children's Hospital. It was an important cause for me to support, as I recalled years before visiting a hospital in Memphis, as professional sports teams have their players do. I remember seeing the little kids there so sick; some of them with no hair, and they needed so much help. It's one thing to see all that on TV and quite another to walk in there and experience it with all of one's senses—to see it in person, to hear it, to smell it, and to feel it. It was a very emotional thing for me. I wanted to reach out and help every single one of those beautiful children, so when the opportunity to participate in the telethon arose, I jumped right in.

Back on the trail that year, I moved Linda to Tennessee while she was pregnant. Once we arrived in Memphis, I was back on the bus again—the darned Old Iron Lung—playing games on the road. In November while I was gone, Linda went into labor. She was in a brand-new town with which she was totally unfamiliar when our son Dave decided it was time to make his appearance. Not knowing where to go, a bunch of the hockey wives, including one of the prominent wives, Iris Keller, and Linda piled into someone's car and drove around until they found Memphis Methodist Hospital. However, I heard that they had to make a few laps around the place before they found the way in that night. This being Linda's first child and having no close relations there to coach her through the process made the whole ordeal quite frightening for Linda, especially when there were complications.

Back then, communicating was not easy, there were no phones on the Old Iron Lung, and even if there had been, the clubs did not give players the consideration that they do today. If you were on the road and there was a family emergency or if your wife was having a baby, it didn't matter. You just kept playing.

The next day, when I finally received the news of Linda having the baby, I telephoned her right away. I was, as I imagine all first-time fathers are, very nervous. When I called, the nurse awakened Linda, and I said, "So, I heard you had a baby."

"I did?" she asked. Apparently, the anesthesia they administered to her because of complications worked quite well. The staff there took wonderful care of her and told me that Linda had given birth to a healthy baby boy. We named him David.

During that time, I was on the road playing in places like Tulsa, Oklahoma, and Omaha, so by the time we got back to Memphis, I think Dave was at least three weeks old. That's the kind of sacrifice we had to go through trying to make it to the NHL; you sacrificed your time and your family's time, while being forced to make compromises you didn't want to make. When I finally got home, it was quite a sight and joy to be able to see and hold my first child. It's hard to explain the range of emotions that come with those moments. I felt relieved to finally be there, excited to meet my son and overwhelmed at the new responsibility I was facing: to have that little, innocent baby rely on me to provide for his well-being.

In addition to the personal changes our growing family was going through, being in the south was another amazing experience, introducing us to a new culture, new foods, and a slightly different way of life. We are fortunate to have been able to enjoy that beautiful area and for one of our children to be born there.

It was also exciting to be a part of introducing ice hockey to a new area of the country and to so many people who had never seen ice or skates in person. The people there were so kind and receptive to us and the game. For an area that was so unfamiliar to the sport, it was very fulfilling to be drawing in maybe seven or eight thousand people to our games, which was a pretty good draw at that time. They seemed to love the game, and the only thing I regret is that we never got Elvis Presley out to skate with us. We did, however, see him going into his home at Graceland in 1965. It was quite the event to see him in his pink Cadillac with his entourage and all.

We all worked very hard on that team throughout the whole season, and consequently, we had a pretty good one there in Memphis. I was one of the top scorers with forty-one goals that year. Even though it was difficult playing down in the minors, we maintained and made a little bit of money. We definitely had something to build on, so we went into the off-season with a good feeling.

Linda and I returned home to Canada, and I went back to looking for a job so that I could support my growing family. Having a baby who was only about six months old brought about new pressures. I needed to go home to get a job to pay our rent and put food on the table, but one of the hardest parts of going home was getting there. The team gave us very little money to get home—certainly not any additional funds for those of us traveling internationally—so that was rather disheartening. I'm sure those practices forced many otherwise capable players to give up on their dream and drop out of the leagues, which would have been quite a blow to a young man's ego.

There were a lot of personal trials and tribulations, but at that time, the NHL wouldn't part with much money even though they were drawing sixteen to seventeen thousand fans to a game. As far as the players were concerned, they were just a number in the organization, and that was it. These business practices ran quite contrary to what I had been taught and experienced in my corner of the world, so I was consistently confounded at how shabbily we were all treated. The compassion was blatantly absent.

1965/66 Pittsburgh Hornets

The 1965-66 season found me playing for the Pittsburgh Hornets again. This was a good group that I was used to playing with, which made the transition a bit easier. Linda and I both liked Pittsburgh, but as Linda was busy filling our home-team roster, she spent most of her time in Canada. Our daughter Nadine was born while I was in Pittsburgh. Just as it was with Dave, it wasn't until a few weeks later that we had a break from game play long enough for us to get home and finally hold my precious first daughter in my arms. Wow. A whole new flood of emotions comes with becoming a father to a daughter. It wouldn't be too long before I learned that those same emotions arose each time we were blessed with a new baby, regardless of if it was a boy or girl. Each new life presents itself as a beautiful, blank canvas, loaned to us to watch over while they are here on Earth with us. However, the bonding time was short but sweet, and soon, I was back on the road.

1966/67 Memphis Red Wings

The second time I was sent to Memphis was a little easier because we had been there before, and the people were acclimated to hockey. We had previously spent a lot of time educating the fans about what the game of hockey was all about, and they seemed to gravitate toward it after a while because of the aggressiveness and the fighting in addition to the game itself. They were more knowledgeable the second year, and again we had a pretty good season under coach Jim Peters. We were playing against teams from St. Louis, Oklahoma, Omaha, Houston, and Tulsa with some pretty decent hockey players who later moved up to the NHL. We had a pretty good season in Memphis; again I scored quite a few goals, was the leading scorer, trying hard to make it to the big league. The NHL was the real goal for each and every one of us, and having that in common made the time traveling together in the bus and on planes that much easier. In addition to wanting to take good care of our families, we all shared that common goal, so we understood each other.

In 1967, we were playing against the Montreal Canadiens in an exhibition game in Hull, Quebec. I was hit by another big defenseman and knocked out clean. When I came to and got my breath back, I started spitting blood, so I was rushed to the hospital to make sure it was not a ruptured spleen or anything serious. Fortunately, it was not, and I was released after several days in the hospital. I never asked questions about what the injuries were, I just followed their directions. I survived another injury.

Sometimes when I would have to fill out medical forms or talk to doctors about my medical history, I couldn't speak about it with any sort of accuracy because I really didn't know. Sometimes they looked at me strangely, but I never felt like I needed to know the extent my injuries or even what they were. That was better left for the medical staff and trainers. I just did what they told me to do and moved on. My job was to win hockey games, not fix broken bodies.

On hockey teams, as I imagine it is amongst most professional sports teams, your teammates become a sort of surrogate family, especially back in those days when we would spend so much time together on the bus and in hotels, not like today where players fly in on their own jets and helicopters. We were in close quarters and were a tight-knit community. We could commiserate with each other, knowing how hard it was to keep your family happy while you were away, especially for those who had left little ones behind. We had to do that amongst ourselves, for there would be no complaining around coaches or management, to be sure.

The Memphis Wings ended up losing in the playoffs that year, but we had a good team, and we played well together, so it was, as always, difficult to say goodbye to our home there. Being in the playoffs was fun, and we made a little bit of extra money for getting there. It was quite an experience to play hockey in the south, making friends with the southerners, talking like, "Y'all come back now, ya hear?" and eating a lot of hominy grits. Next season would bring us something quite different, as it would be the expansion year.

Cincinnati Gardens Arena (1963)

Pittsburgh Arena (1965)

Hull-Ottawa, 5; Syracuse, 2
First period
1—Hull-Ottawa. Beaudin (Carter) 5.41
 Penalty: Fizzell. 4 33
Second period
2—Hull-Ottawa. Carter
 (White, Harper) · 1 06
3—Hull-Ottawa, Carter (Labrosse) 16 21
4—Hull-Ottawa. Rodger (Ellett) 18 25
 Penalties Ellett, 3 59 Harper. 10.51;
Robazzo, 15.28. Labrosse, 19.06.
Third period
5—Syracuse, Lalande
 (Robazzo. Hall) ·· 1.12
6—Hull-Ottawa, B. McCreary
 (Senior) -------- 1.28
7—Syracuse, Hall
 (Kuryluk, Harris) ... · 17 18
 Penalties: Polano, 1.53; Labrosse,
7.48.
Stops
Crozier 11 7 3—21
Wakely-Beaudin 11 8 10—29

Goalie and forward stat sheet

Norm with a Pats trophy

Chapter Four

TIME FOR THE BIG SHOW

1967/68 St. Louis Blues/Kansas City Blues

1967-68 was the next season that rushed upon us, and it would be a very memorable season for me. With the NHL's expansion came six new teams: the California Seals, Los Angeles Kings, Minnesota North Stars, Philadelphia Flyers, Pittsburgh Penguins, and the St. Louis Blues. In June of 1967, I was drafted eleventh by the Blues in the expansion draft. I got the letter that summer that I was to report to St. Louis for training camp. I would become one of the original St. Louis Blues! Linda and I were so excited. This was the NHL, Baby!

That September, I drove to St. Louis to attend training camp, and, of all people involved, who is there but my nemesis, Scotty Bowman. Lynn Patrick, the GM, who was much easier for me to deal with, was originally the coach, but he resigned mid-season and was replaced by none other than Mr. Bowman. As I recall, the arena there was big and beautiful, capable of seating many fans. I had a good camp there, and after camp I went to my meeting with Lynn Patrick and Scotty Bowman. I started talking, and they told me to come back the next day.

That night in the lobby, an agent started talking to me about contracts—how he could negotiate based on similar players, right wings, and such. He introduced himself as Alan Eagleson, and after listening to him talk, I declined the assistance he offered and told him I would get back to him if I felt I needed to. I had heard he was going around talking to guys at different training camps and what he said made sense, especially given the trouble I always had with Scotty Bowman. I thought perhaps an agent like Eagleson could find out what Bowman didn't like about me and what I needed to do to win his approval.

41

Even though I was inexperienced in the business world and obviously not the greatest contract negotiator, something just didn't feel right about that guy. I ended up signing my own contract—an okay one. Although Eagleson's bargaining power at the time may have pulled down a much higher contract for me, I am fortunate to have not signed him on as my agent. Many others who did ended up paying him exorbitant fees and having funds embezzled by him. He eventually spent time in jail for his crimes, and I am thankful I listened to the voice inside of me and chose not to associate with him.

Contract bull aside, there was a different breed of butterflies in my stomach as I entered the locker room. I looked around until I found my name, and there was my sweater (what we used to call them in Canada, now called a jersey), number 21, and my equipment waiting for me. Back then, we didn't get to choose the numbers on our jerseys, they were assigned to us, and we got what we got. I was always fine with that; I was just happy to be putting on a team jersey and playing hockey. (I'm different today, as I now like to choose my numbers. I tend to like higher numbers and for some reason lean toward odd numbers. Today I would choose number 77, as that is my age and just because I think it's a good number.)

Opening Day, October 11, 1967, was the birth of the St. Louis Blues, and it was my father's birthday! What an episode, being involved with opening the team. I recall the beautiful voice of Anna Marie Alberghetti echoing through the arena as she sang *The Birth of the Blues* and the national anthem. It was also the birth of my formal NHL career, so a fantastically momentous occasion for our family all the way around. I'm sure that was a special birthday for my father that year.

The season got off to a pretty good start, and man was it fun playing in the NHL with a lot of the players who had been drafted from other NHL teams, like Glenn Hall and Al Arbour, as well as others who had first played in the minors. I will never forget what a great town St. Louis was; the townspeople were so welcoming, and the fans were, and still are, exceptional. It was a great experience, very fun, but the elation was short-lived.

Halfway through the season, I was dispatched to the Kansas City Blues in the Central Hockey League. Not a surprise given that Scotty Bowman was at the helm. Playing in Kansas City was good though; we were playing under coach Doug Harvey, who would later be inducted into the NHL Hall of Fame. He had played in Montreal for many years, and he was a highly skilled coach, so it felt good to play for him.

While I was with Kansas City, we flew into Oklahoma City around 2:30 a.m. on the night before a game. My roomie, Roger Picard, said he was going to bed, but I wanted to get breakfast so that I could sleep in until about noon. A couple of other guys and I went to eat, and when I arrived back at our room about an hour later, stuffed like a Thanksgiving turkey, the door was open. Not thinking much of it, I took my tie off and went into the bathroom, and there was some strange guy standing there. I didn't know what the heck he was doing. I was in shock, really. I asked him what he was doing and when he had no explanation, I grabbed him and then he threatened to shoot me. I let go of him and yelled for Roger, who in the off-season was a police officer, but I couldn't wake him. Before I knew what had happened, the burglar ran out the door, and I foolishly followed him. If he had really had a gun, I might have been a hero, but what good is a dead hero? Still, being a young, tough guy who didn't have any money to spare, I chased him down the hall, and he ran out the exit. I caught up to him there and gave him a good kick. He almost went over the railing but managed to catch himself which was probably a good thing since we were about four stories high. He didn't end up making off with anything, but maybe a bit of my pride and hopefully a seriously bruised leg.

It was a very frightening experience, and although I couldn't sleep that night, I had a job to do the following day. Not everything in the NHL was as great as I thought it would be, and if Linda didn't worry enough about me on the ice, now she was going to worry about me off the ice, too. Ah, life's challenges.

The latter part of the season, early 1968, found me called back to St. Louis for the Stanley Cup playoffs for what was an extremely exciting time in my life. After beating out the Minnesota North Stars, we made it to the final round where, although we were outgunned and ended up losing in four games to the Montreal Canadiens, as a new team, we had exceeded expectations; we were a powerhouse. We had a great goaltender in Glenn Hall. It was an amazing experience given the fans and all their enthusiasm; every night was quite a scene. It was good for the whole family, a shining highlight in my career.

At the end of that season, I had another run-in with Scotty Bowman, and while I know most people sing the praises of Scotty and negative talk seems to not make its way out of tight-knit groups and their private conversations, I have a different story to tell—and I'm not afraid to be honest and lay it all out there. Scotty seemed to go out of his way to needle me, and I saw him do it to several others as well. I never understood why, but there is another incident that stands out to me, which occurred during the Finals.

I was at a game but not suited up. In the dressing room, players were talking about our teammate Dickie Moore who wasn't feeling well. After a while, everyone was dressed and ready to warm up on the ice. I left the dressing room and went upstairs to watch the game, and all of a sudden, I heard my name over the PA system, announcing for me to head to the dressing room immediately. I was so excited; I thought I was going to get to play that night in this important game, and I couldn't get downstairs fast enough. I sprinted to the locker room, and there Bowman stood, telling me it was all okay; I wasn't needed. He was just messing with me, like he did with players, and this was just a small taste of what it was like to be under the Bowman leadership.

1968/69 Buffalo Bisons

Training camp for the Blues for the 1968-69 season was in St. Andrew's By-the-Sea, New Brunswick, Canada: lobster country. Being from Saskatchewan, lobster wasn't common, as had to be shipped in from the eastern provinces. So, at twenty-six years old, I tried my first lobster. It was okay. Training camp that year lasted about three weeks, and I went through the same contract routine with Scotty Bowman and Lynn Patrick. Although I signed a contract, I wasn't put on the Blues roster. Instead I was loaned to the Buffalo Bisons of the American Hockey League under coach Fred Shero. The Bisons were affiliated with the New York Rangers, but I had been loaned to them by the Blues. We had a strong team, and we only lost eighteen games all season. We had quality guys on our team, like Walt Tkachuk, Brad Park, and Gilles Villemure—lots of great players.

Oddly enough, when being asked by fans about favorite numbers and favorite places to play, etc., I recall that one of my favorite uniforms and logos was the Pepsi logo we wore in Buffalo. I heard that the AHL didn't like the affiliation, and that was years before heavy marketing hit all facets of major sports franchises, but there was something about that logo I liked.

The team was looking good, and I was feeling good, so come October, I went to get Linda and our two kids. She was pregnant with our third child. We didn't waste any time loading up our bench—that's for sure. We drove our car to Buffalo and got settled on the Canadian side in Fort Erie, Ontario, which was about fifteen minutes from the arena. I was warmly welcomed by Fred Shero, whom they called The Fog. He was a very good coach, easy to play for if you worked hard.

Our son Greg was born while I was on the road playing in Baltimore. During the game, the coaches called me over and delivered the news that I was the father of another son. I was ecstatic. I took that abundance of energy and translated it into celebratory goals right there on the ice, that very night. That momentum seemed to carry me through that season.

We were great up to the playoffs, but then our parent team, the Rangers, were in a dilemma. They had four or five injured players, so what do you think happened? They called up three or four of our best players, which absolutely decimated our team. Naturally, we lost out in four straight to the Hershey Bears, who had a hot goaltender. Losing those players was a big deal to us—talk about killing team morale. The remaining players were very discouraged, in part because we worked so hard to make it that far. We felt like we would have had a chance to take home the Calder Cup trophy, only to have that opportunity taken away from us. Again, this resulted in a significant financial loss to us players, costing me about $3,000 in bonuses, which was a lot of money at the time. We did get bonuses for making the playoffs, but winning would have likely tripled those amounts.

The Rangers ended up losing in, I believe, the first round. I understand that they needed our players, but why the organization felt the need to turn their backs on guys working so hard for them surprises me to this day. However, in the end I believe it was their greed that led to the rebel league: the World Hockey Association, the thorn in their side that forced the NHL to improve its ways and become the premier league that it is today. I guess it was all worth it, even though the load was unfairly placed squarely on the backs of young guys like me. Even for those who are too young to have watched the inception of this new league, reading about the buzz and the excitement in the daily newspapers was something we can all learn from.

At that time, the NHL was like a petulant teenager—moody and impossible sometimes, but they're yours and you love them just the same. The NHL went through growing pains and learned along the way. This was just a difficult yet necessary phase.

After losing to the Hershey Bears at the end of the season, naturally Linda, our kids, and I were all ready to go back home to the calm consistency and our family in Regina, Saskatchewan. We loaded up a trailer with our belongings, piled into our car, and with the trailer in tow, left Buffalo—I think it was the first week of April. About 150 miles out of Buffalo our car broke down. We ended up hitchhiking back to town, leaving the car and all of our belongings in the middle of nowhere. We went back to our empty place in Buffalo, after which I flew Linda and the kids to Canada—first to Toronto, then to Winnipeg, Linda alone and pregnant with three small kids. My brother Alain picked them up in Winnipeg and drove them to Regina, which was a day of travel in itself. It was quite an ordeal for Linda, I am sure, but she is a tough lady and not one to complain. We had the car towed to a garage only to find out that the motor was shot. I ended up having to hang around there for a couple of weeks waiting for the parts to fix the car to get in so I could continue my journey back to Canada and find a part-time job.

One of those jobs was modeling. When I got back home to Regina, one of my friends told me he needed someone to model clothes and asked if I would be interested in doing it. It didn't seem like a very masculine thing to do, and I had never modeled, but I needed money to support my family, so I said, "I think I can do it."

I modeled for the Hudson Bay Company: one of the oldest retail stores in Canada. Some of the pictures required the use of a pipe as a prop, and back then I did occasionally smoke a pipe, so it was fitting that I would have a pipe in the pictures.

I did not get rich, but the modeling gig paid the bills for the summer, and it was an enjoyable experience.

1969/70, 1970/71, 1971/72 Cleveland Barons, Minnesota North Stars

After leaving Buffalo, I think I was purchased by the Minnesota North Stars who had a working agreement with the Cleveland Barons of the American Hockey League. We had a decent team with the North Stars organization. In the middle of the season, I was the top scorer, so the North Stars called me up to play for them with players such as J. P. Parise, Cesare Maniago, and Gump Worsley. There we had a decent team. I think they had one of the first American players, Tom Williams. Everyone else on that team was from Canada. After several months, they sent me back to Cleveland to finish out the season where we ended up making the playoffs. Eventually we lost, but Cleveland was a solid hockey town. They'd had hockey since about the 1920s. The arena would draw probably eight or nine thousand people. I spent three years playing for those teams, going between the Cleveland Barons and the Minnesota North Stars. Linda and I really liked Cleveland; it was beautiful, and the people treated us very well. We would both like to visit that area again sometime soon.

Our youngest child, Carrie, was the only one born in the off-season, so I was present (at least in the same area code) when she was born. When Linda went into labor, she was a well-seasoned baby-deliverer. I drove her to the hospital and began my wait on the boring side of the cold, forbidding steel doors of the maternity ward. When I was given the news that I was the poppa of another baby girl, I was ready with the cigars. Funny to think that you could smoke in hospitals back then. In fact, you were pretty much *expected* to light up when the good news arrived. My, how times have changed.

While life on the home front was very satisfying, one thing that did disappoint us about hockey in Cleveland was when Nick Mileti built the new Coliseum in between Cleveland and Akron. I suppose they were trying to fill the 20,000 plus seats by drawing from two metropolitan areas, but it just struck me as a bad idea from the start. Those were two very different cities, and you can't bridge rivalries by simply forcing people to go to neutral territory. Cleveland was partial to having its own stadium, and I heard the new stadium even had design flaws, as well as traffic troubles. After a short time, it folded. Fortunately, they built what was then called Gund Arena in downtown Cleveland and moved the operation back home.

The failed arena is another example of how ownership in those days failed their constituents, their players, and their customers. The coaches seemed well respected. I'm sure they all got along because if the coach was successful, the whole organization was seen as successful. The coaches wanted to help the players more than they did at the time, but they really had no say; their hands were tied. They had the attitude that they did what they could and that's all there was.

I've learned that professional teams in every sport are much the same way today as far as helping players. Players are commodities like cattle, and I caution anyone contemplating pursuing a professional sports career to be ready for the heartache that often accompanies a venture into that area—especially before reaching the top tier of their leagues. Contracts can be very one-sided toward the organization, especially in the minor leagues. Players can be released at a moment's notice without compensation and really no humane consideration. It is of vital importance to have not only a good contract and good representation, but also an awareness of what can happen to young players if a team feels they are not performing well. One day you can be riding high and the next being kicked out of your temporary housing with nowhere to go.

As players, how did we deal with those pressures? Again, with the pranks. Just boys in men's bodies, I suppose. It seems we like to gravitate toward fire. Usually, one of the players would start reading a newspaper while we were on the bus or in a hotel lobby when all of a sudden, their newspaper was in flames. Talk about news "hot off the press." Some of us were very stealth at sneaking up with a lit match, but sometimes those pranks took a turn like my Halloween adventure. I was once involved in a "hot news" situation *on a plane*! I won't mention any names, but he was my centerman. Talk about a frightening situation when your newspaper is on fire on a plane. Imagine the FAA getting ahold of that story. We would have been banned for life.

Fun aside, when I was playing professionally, I'm sure we lost a lot of otherwise competent and even exceptional players because of poor treatment by the league. I often wonder how different the sport would be if we had been able to hold on to some of those guys that couldn't take the constant change, the flux, and the uncertainty. The league could undoubtedly have been better; they would have had a much larger group of players from which to pick. Those of us who stayed and toughed it out just worked hard to continue to get better, to win championships, and to make money. The guys who came from families who were more well off were obviously able to ride out the tough times and make it to training camp without the stress of having to financially support their families.

While I was in Cleveland, I was lucky to spend a couple of years working with coach John Muckler. He was also our manager. He coached the Minnesota North Stars later on and went on to coach the Edmonton Oilers to several Cup playoffs. He was a good coach, and I'm fortunate to have spent some time with him.

However, I did not make it through my time with the Barons without injuring myself. After a grueling hit, I had several broken ribs. Coach Muckler asked me if I could play, and for the first time, I had to say "no." I couldn't play in that condition. It was right before the playoffs, so after a few days, and under a doctor's direction, they decided to freeze my ribs (they shot them up with something to numb them) for the duration of the playoffs. It was still very painful, to say the least. By the end of the playoffs, which was seven games, my whole side was black. Bad idea.

We also didn't have the resources available today as far as physical training regimens, equipment, dietary knowledge, or advice, but somehow, we made it all work. We were tuned in to our bodies. We ate what our bodies demanded, which for some was a lot of beer, and we got our workouts by doing good, old-fashioned hard labor back at home in the off-season. We also all seemed to have one more thing in common: the desire to be on the ice. I don't see that in many professional athletes in other sports. How many football players live to be on the field playing ball every day? How many basketball players crave their time on the wood court every single day? Hockey players are obsessed—*obsessed*, nothing less. Speeding along in the cold air at a speed many times that at which one can run is addicting, so training doesn't seem like training; it's a necessity; it's life-sustaining.

Sometimes things that seem necessary and have, perhaps, become habits are not always the best things for us—especially in large doses. As I was writing this book, I was apprehensive about discussing the darker side of the sport. Those events happened decades ago, but they are still relevant to my career. If someone today can relate to my predicament, and it gives them valuable insight, provokes thought, or helps them make a good decision, it is worthy of the discussion.

Given my disappointment at some facets of yesteryear's hockey, even if I had the knowledge then that I have today, would I have kept playing? Probably. The love of the game was just so instilled in me that I didn't know anything else. In addition, I found myself married with kids, having to provide for my family in the only way I knew how. At one pivotal time in my career when I was in the latter portion of my twenties, I felt I just had to keep going, to keep pushing on to make it back into the NHL, with a plan in the back of my mind to move into coaching down the road. When you're twenty-eight with four kids, you tend to stick with what you know.

Then, as if by divine intervention, stories began breaking of a new league that was going to be formed. The buzz was electric, and its spark changed the lives of many for the better.

St. Lous puck (October 28, 1967)

Blues first score sheet

Martial Beaudin holding Norm's daughter, Carrie (1970)

Chapter Five

A NEW BRAND OF HOCKEY, W.H.A. STYLE

On the ice, when you meet a tough competitor, you must step up your game, or you will lose—plain and simple. Business is no different. Competition drives improvement. When the World Hockey Association (WHA) was formed to challenge the NHL, a new game was on. Who was behind this? One was a guy from California named Dennis Murphy—quite the legend. He was instrumental in starting the ABA and also the AFL. There was an abundance of players, and salaries were so low that the WHA could tell the field was ripe for the picking. Why not give it a go? I haven't heard the whole backstory; I mean, gossip abounds, and countless articles were in the papers, but the media gets things wrong from time to time, so I didn't listen to all the chatter. That was until my phone rang… and rang… and rang.

At first, it was just friends and players calling to ask what I knew about the new league. When I was contacted by several owners and managers of teams that were being assembled, it started to sound like the new league might actually come to fruition. They wanted to talk to me. I was in demand, in the power position, which was something new for me.

I didn't talk to the other players about what I was hearing, and they didn't talk to me, either. We all just kind of kept things under wraps, even though nothing in our contracts prohibited us from talking to potential competitors because the league at that time was too arrogant to believe anyone would come in and challenge them or shake up the status quo. In early 1972, I believe it was Bill Robinson, the head of the Winnipeg Jets, who started calling players and having meetings. Bill ended up coming unannounced to Cleveland (I guess they conducted as many of these meetings on the sly as possible) and asked to meet with me. He asked to talk about the new league. I thought, *why not?* So, I agreed to meet with him.

Our meeting went down soon thereafter; I think we met in some back alley in Cleveland, where no one could see us. Even though we weren't doing anything wrong, if I would have been seen, the team I was with may have found a way to suspend me—or who knows what at that time. During our meeting, Bill outlined the proposed teams, and he talked about the new players that they were talking to, those who were interested in making the jump to the WHA. I can't deny that it was wildly exciting—exciting to have those proposals out there, to know that something big was coming around, shaking up the stoic league and laying down opportunities for so many great players. It was such a contrast to the NHL as everything with the WHA was open and on the table, and you weren't berated for opening your mouth.

Later that season, I think it was right before the playoffs, we started reading headlines about a new professional hockey league being formed vs. the NHL. At that time, it was just speculation and rumors coming out in the papers until all of a sudden Bobby Hull's name came into the picture, which made it all that much more interesting for the players. That alone made the league viable. Then Gordie Howe's name started coming up, and Gerry Cheevers' name was dropped as well.

As the buzz continued to grow, I, after much discussion with Linda, committed to going to Winnipeg to talk to them and act as my own agent. Of course, we (Cleveland) were going to be in the playoffs, so it would have to wait until after that. I think that year we lost in the first round. However, it was going to pan out; there was a new spring in everyone's step, and though it was largely just nervous energy, even in the NHL there was an added excitement at the possibility of something big happening.

After the season ended, we arranged a meeting between the Winnipeg people and me. The players on my team didn't seem surprised at any of the events as they occurred. I have no idea who had been talked to and who hadn't. The hockey guys around me just didn't talk about contracts and things like that at the time, and especially me, being a generally reserved guy. Well, we all just kept things to ourselves. People were overall much more private at that time, so not talking about it didn't seem out of place. Personally, I had to keep it quiet because if the new league didn't go, I couldn't afford to burn my bridges and end my career over nothing, which was the same for most everyone around me. I also didn't want to see the league damaged. I love hockey; I live for hockey; I bleed hockey; and I didn't want to have any hand in damaging the sport, only enhancing it.

We finally met towards the end of April when I flew to Winnipeg and met with Bill Robinson. We had dinner and talked about the league. They talked about getting Bobby Hull, and although he hadn't signed yet, I was intrigued. I didn't have an agent, friend, or relative helping me out, but I sat down and negotiated a three-year contract stating that I would go to Winnipeg. It was a substantial contract. I think it was on April 26th that I signed the deal—the deal that changed my whole life, of course, along with the lives of so many others.

As the news started coming out, I was surprised at how many players jumped. The news was crazy, and owners were frenzied. I guess there were a lot of other guys that had received the same treatment as me, and although they didn't complain about it, they were happy to have this remedy laid out before them. It was a bittersweet payday, leaving the NHL, but the emphasis was on the *sweet*, for sure.

Over the years the WHA was in existence, many players made the move over from the NHL. One need look no further than the Wikipedia entry for Dave Keon to see some of the drama involved with manipulation of a player by an NHL owner. These stories emphasize, italicize, and underscore how much players had to look forward to by making the switch. If things had been so great where they were, so many guys wouldn't have left. We were all sick of owners and managers telling us when to go to bed and what to eat—and for such little pay. When I think back, we were young and making some brave decisions, but I didn't experience any backlash, nor did I hear of any being dished out against anyone else I knew personally. We were just free to breathe as we wished. All the time-worn sayings come to mind: we reached the light at the end of the tunnel; the burden was lifted; a new day had dawned; I could go on and on. Man, was it a breath of fresh air.

Things didn't go off without a hitch or two, and there was quite a bit of tension. In June or so of that year, Bobby Hull had signed but wasn't going to be able to play because of some contract issues—or something along those lines. (Don't quote me; I'm not a lawyer.) Bobby had to actually go to court to defend his right to make a living. Litigating in court isn't a place anyone who I know wants to be, especially a hockey player. Quite out of our realm of comfort. Bobby stuck it out, however, and when he finally was able to make it official, they made it a big deal. We had all been watching very intently, and the league had to get Bobby, so it was a *very* big deal. They paid him the big bucks. It was the deal of the century! It was great to see. I didn't know him before that, but we finally met when the league was formed and the teams organized. I had played *against* him before. The first time I saw Bobby was when the Blues played the Blackhawks. In that game, Bobby scored two goals, and we lost two to four—so he didn't start off on my good side. I mentioned it to him later, and we had a good laugh over it. It was so much better to be playing on the same side of the puck as him. I had no idea that I would play with him on the *same line* until it came to fruition. We were already into the season when Judge Higginbotham— his name has always stuck with me—declared that Bobby was free to sign and play in the WHA. What a hero, that Judge Higginbotham.

Starting a major-league franchise is no small deal, and things got switched around here and there, but we ended up starting with twelve teams—six each in two divisions, Eastern and Western. The divisions were broken down as follows:

Eastern	Western
Cleveland Crusaders	Alberta Oilers
New England Whalers	Chicago Cougars
New York Raiders	Houston Aeros
Ottawa Nationals	Los Angeles Sharks
Philadelphia Blazers	Minnesota Fighting Saints
Quebec Nordiques	Winnipeg Jets

Training camp that first year was as good as training camp can get, for me, at least. It was held in Kenora, Ontario—a gorgeous resort town. It was a good camp, and we carried our excitement from Winnipeg to the camp.

When the regular season finally arrived, our first night playing was an away game in the Big Apple, New York, in none other than The Madison Square Garden against the Raiders. There is just something magical about The Garden. It was indeed a thrill and an honor to play there. I had been to New York before, but that trip was something special. We walked the streets, and this rural Canadian boy was in awe at the towering buildings, the never-ending streams of people, and all the city had to offer. We ate great food there, with the whole team going out to eat like ravenous carnivores before the game. I had the usual steak, baked potato, and vegetables. I didn't need a trainer or dietician to tell me that my body needed just that to perform. We won that night—six to four—in front of a sell-out crowd.

Opening night at home was tremendous. I arrived at the game early, as is the custom for me and most guys I know, and walked into a locker room that looked like no other I had been in. As the bustle of the crowd outside began to filter in, I pulled on my jersey, number 11, a number that became quite iconic in my life after that. While I didn't choose my numbers, it seems that throughout the years and across teams, I almost always had a 1 in mine. Number 10, 11, 21, 17—there is a common thread that I never recognized until I started writing this book.

The fans in Winnipeg were enthusiastic to the point of being boisterous. They conveyed a fantastic energy, even though we all felt the void of not having Bobby Hull there on the ice. His absence tamped down the mood of the players and the fans because we had to begin playing without our star. I recall the stadium, grand walls sheltering us from the elements, the feel of the crisp new sweater (jersey), the portrait of the Queen hanging in the rafters, and the sweet sound of our national anthem "O Canada," bellowing proudly from the mouths of excited fans and echoing across the walls around us. Linda and the kids were all present, and my whole family was listening to the game on the radio.

Winnipeg, as a town, wasn't happy with Bobby's absence after all the fanfare involved with signing him, but when he eventually stepped onto the ice and started playing, a new era of hockey started. The Luxury Line was born. Bobby Hull, Chris Bordeleau, and I earned the moniker "The Luxury Line" or "Century Line" for being the highest-scoring line in the WHA, with each player scoring over 100 points. We started playing and didn't look back. It was like poetry in motion. We had great chemistry—the kind you can't develop—it just takes on a life of its own. We each had an uncanny ability to know what the other two were going to do, and we capitalized on that intuition all season. People would say it was like we had eyes in the back of our heads. I don't know if it was the excitement of the whole deal that heightened our awareness or what, but it was a working unit like none we had seen before. Man, was it was FUN!

We used that symbiosis to carry us right to the playoffs, through the first round against the Minnesota Fighting Saints and through the second round playing the Houston Aeros. We ended up falling short in the Avco Cup championship round against the New England Whalers that year, the inaugural year of the Winnipeg Jets.

In addition to bringing this level of hockey to Winnipeg, going to Winnipeg was the nexus of our personal life. At that time, we as players were respected more than ever because the owners needed *us*. They had put out a lot of money to get players, and we were treated well. Most of the time, when you asked for money to move or something, they were happy to oblige. For example, in 1972 after returning to Regina from Cleveland, they paid the moving expenses when it was time to go to Winnipeg. Not something heard of before that! We were able to get a home in Winnipeg and moved there that August. Training camp started in September—the first training camp for the Winnipeg Jets. Carrie was two years old, and although there's no way she could have known what was going on, I swear I could see an extra twinkle in her eye when she heard the news.

It was quite a transition going to Winnipeg from where we had been. It was a new era not only for us, but also for the hockey world as a whole. One of the main differences was the formation and presence of the players' association. Comprised of the players of the WHA, we suddenly had a united voice. As a team, we held a meeting, and I was elected as one of the two player reps. From there, the representatives from all teams would gather at meetings, and if there were issues or grievances, we had an outlet in which we could express and resolve them. Wow! That was so refreshing; it was like we were on another planet. Now we weren't just athletes; we were career men in charge of our own business, so-to-speak, and man, did it feel good. We went from boys to men with the swipe of a pen.

Being a player representative was a significant honor. We were nominated by the players and had the privilege of being able to attend meetings in places like Puerto Rico, Las Vegas, and Mexico. The meetings were mini-vacations at great destinations. At the meetings, we usually found we were all coming from a common viewpoint. We would organize our issues and take them to the higher-ups. By working together, we created an atmosphere of mutual respect that is still present in the sport today.

With the new league came new responsibilities in regard to public relations. The WHA did a good job of promoting its teams and players. I recall one particular photo shoot in which the photographer, Gerry Hart, wanted to get a shot of me in full gear, coming around the net with a puck. Photographers weren't usually down on the ice with us, but he wanted to get the best pictures possible, so he was there in the action. I did as he asked, pretended to shoot, and raised my stick. I guess the fake was a little too good, as he got scared that I was flinging a puck at him. He started to fall, threw the camera, and landed on the ice flat on his back, followed by the airborne camera, which landed with a thud on his chest. Thankfully it didn't land on the ice, or it would have been history. He even managed to get the shot before he fell. It made for a great picture, which I still have.

During this time, the players picked the captains, and there wasn't all the PR stuff to consider that is involved today. Managers and coaches may have voiced their support for one guy or another, but it was still up to the team to choose who they felt was their best leader. The additional responsibilities for the captains were to lead, to try to iron out differences, and to set an example. It works well, as there is a leader both on and off the ice, who understands what is going on and brings it all together.

It felt so good to play for the new team, in a new town. Winnipeg was (and still is) a great hockey city. They graciously supported the team and the entire league. Everyone there knew hockey, so they related well to the players. I very much enjoyed playing for and living in Winnipeg. We made a lot of great friends there, and of course, winning didn't hurt. When you're scoring big-time, it feels good all over. When you win, you don't feel the cold, even in Winnipeg. The sun shines brighter, and the food tastes better.

Life off the ice was good; our family was centered, and we felt at home. We were in closer proximity to our family in Saskatchewan, and my family members were able to come to our games, as well as my friends whom I had played with back in the 1950s. They could fill a section at those games—what a great experience.

Looking back, I sometimes feel that not all our decisions were the correct ones, even though they felt so at the time. Despite the early trepidation, signing with Winnipeg was a good move on our part. I gambled and rolled the dice, and it paid off for so many people.

My sons were excited as well, and they began playing hockey a bit more seriously. They were tough players—and thankfully so because some of that strength was needed off the ice. One winter I had picked up Greg from practice, and as we drove home, I gunned our big North American car (I can't recall exactly which model, but it was big) to get up the icy driveway. I got out and opened the garage door (no electric opener at the time), got back in the car, and as I revved the engine and started driving into the garage, I heard screaming and felt a thump. Oh, Lord, I had run into something. I feared it was the cat and quickly backed up, only to feel another thump. More screaming. I got out of the car and learned that unbeknownst to me, Greg had exited the car while I was opening the garage door, only he had slipped on the ice and ended up with his legs under the car. I had run over my own son! Not once, but twice! A big shout-out and thank you to CCM for making such great equipment because all Greg suffered was some bruising on the legs. His pads had saved him! My ego could have used some pads during that incident, as I suffered some bruising, myself. How does a guy run over his kid? Not only once, but twice? Thankfully, everyone was okay, and we have a good story to tell, right?

I have heard talk about how the WHA was a good thing for some and a bad thing for others. That's always the case with controversial issues, but I firmly believe in my heart that the WHA was the best thing that ever happened to the NHL and to the game of hockey. No single player makes the game, and in this case, it was the players uniting to make a stand and jump ship to the new league. Uniting together under the player association forced the NHL to up their game. Undoubtedly there were mistakes made—jumping headfirst into existing markets was perhaps not the best choice—but overall, it was a success for so many reasons.

As that first year ended with us losing in the championship, it was disappointing, but knowing that you are a part of building something big that makes people feel good made up for that. The Whalers were a good team; they had a lot of ex-NHL players that had jumped to the new league, so it made for great hockey. We drew large crowds and made the league viable. It's ironic, talking about the new league, that the president of the NHL and related figureheads never embraced it. It created jobs and opportunities. It opened up new franchises, new markets, and gave work to countless people, coaches, and trainers in addition to bringing in multiple new talents.

I recall how the then-commissioner of the NHL said the league would never survive, never do this, never do that, and fortunately it did. Then with the new league also came higher salaries. Guys previously making $30,000 per year went to making $200,000 per year. That may sound like a lot of money but in those days, in sports, when your career was going to be that short, you had to make a lifetime of earnings in a short period of time. There weren't all the endorsements and peripheral income sources that are open to athletes todays. With all these successes, the new league won in so many ways.

The second year I think we ended with 100 points and didn't make the playoffs. The way the divisions were aligned, there was one division that was so strong and the first four teams in that division made it, and we were 100 points in a different division, but we didn't make the playoffs. Imagine that! It was devastating. Again, it cost us a lot of money because if you don't make the playoffs, you're missing out on some good payola.

To make up for that loss of potential income, during a couple of off-seasons I sold Chrysler automobiles in Winnipeg. I sold new cars, used cars—whatever they needed sold. I loved the social time and enjoyed talking to clients and making them happy. Anyone who knows much about the car business knows that referrals are a key to success, and I had more referrals than I could handle, thankfully. I say thankfully because learning from some of the other seasoned salesman about all the tricks of the trade was quite eye-opening and not the way I wanted to build relationships or sell cars. Instead, I told my story and related to people on a different level and saw great success in that career.

During one of those off-seasons, I decided that I needed a change of image. That was the seventies and everyone seemed to be growing their hair out so I joined the bunch of them. I grew my hair and even got a perm. I ended up with one of the popular afro styles. Looking back, I probably shouldn't have cut that hair off when the season started because we didn't wear helmets back then, and that thick mass of curly locks certainly would have helped take the place of a helmet and prevented a few headaches.

Prior to that next year of hockey, there wasn't any influence from Europe, but that was part of the idea with the WORLD Hockey Association—to bring in other countries. We did have a couple of players from Sweden on our roster that year, but it wasn't talked about much. We just happened to have a couple of Swedish guys on our team. There was still plenty of old North American hockey being played, though, and even the Swedes joined in. I remember playing a game in San Diego when a brawl erupted. Our goalie, a Swede named Curt Larsson, and Norm Ferguson went at it. Ferguson ripped Larsson's toupee right off and threw it down where it looked like a piece of fresh roadkill. We called them rugs back then, but it didn't look anything like a rug, lying there on the ice.

The toupee removing wasn't limited to Larsson, either. Many people have already heard about the time Bobby Hull had his toupee ripped off, and it was gruesome. He had the thing sewn into his hair so when it was ripped off, it left a bloody mess. But Bobby was one tough son of a gun, and he returned to the ice with a helmet on and finished the game.

Life off the ice was unpredictable. While we were in Winnipeg, we certainly enjoyed a nice celebrity status, which came in handy. One time, we were on a drive, listening to a hockey game on the radio, when the announcer broke into the game with an emergency message for Norm Beaudin to contact emergency services. What? They were talking to *me*? As we were pulling over to turn around, a RCMP (Royal Canadian Mounted Police) vehicle stopped and asked if I was indeed Norm. I said "yes," and he explained to us that Dave had been injured on the ice, and we were needed at the hospital to authorize surgery. The gentleman escorted us straight to the hospital. Wow, talk about service!

The third year I played for the Jets, we had success and again went to the play-offs, but the fourth year was a bigger deal. The hockey world was about to change again. The Winnipeg Jets were the first team to announce training camp in Europe. In September of 1975, we went to Europe to train. Our first stop was in Finland, then on to Sweden, and Czechoslovakia. We played the Swedish national team in Stockholm, and the people there were so receptive—they were outstanding. We had a huge crowd there, got to play the national team, and beat them, like six to three or so. I had a fantastic game that night and scored a couple of goals. It was a memorable camp that would come to benefit me down the road in a way I hadn't expected.

We were well-received and respected there and that's when the influx of European players started to come into North American hockey. With our status in Europe, with training camp promoting hockey and playing in places like Finland and Sweden, we brought back some of those players and they brought with them a different brand of hockey. They weren't grunts. They played with skill, finesse, and speed that was very different from our style of play. From then onward, we had players with skills and not just brawn, so the game evolved to a new level. Other teams had to adapt to our style of play, so they in turn started bringing in players from different countries, including Russia. It's nice to know I was with the Winnipeg Jets who were instrumental in bringing this style of play to the game.

It was my fourth year with the team, and with our abilities, we went to the finals again. We beat the Houston Aeros, who had Gordie Howe, Mark Howe, and Marty Howe—a deal rumored to have been brokered by Gordie's wife, who was one heck of a manager, that's for sure. That was my final season there, and it was a championship year. We swept the final series, taking home the Avco Cup! The fans were elated! WE were elated! It was bedlam all over town! We partied all night long, until the parade the following morning, which started around ten a.m. All the players were there. We rode individually in cars—convertibles, of course. I have no idea how they rounded up that many convertibles in Winnipeg, Canada. When we finally arrived home, the neighbors had placed congratulatory and celebratory signs all over the yard.

It was a winning season in more ways than one. The Jets had changed the whole hockey world for the better and changed the NHL, too, because they started adapting to our style by going to Europe to train and play. The WHA was very innovative in so many respects. I think it's important to share that story for those who haven't heard it. WHA teams were the first teams to have overtime, the first to have shootouts, and the first to bring in European players on a regular basis. Thus, they brought a whole influx of change to the sport. We changed the game in a way that was good for the sport. It was a win-win.

It also wasn't until about 1976 in Winnipeg, after a particularly ugly brawl, that I first wore a helmet. I hated helmets. We all did. However, after I was sucker-punched and took a little unscheduled nap on the ice, I finally decided to wear one. I guess you could say that the guy who hit me finally knocked some sense into me. It was a tough adjustment, but it had to be done. I have worn a helmet ever since, and I won't let anyone play on my ice who doesn't. I think even figure skaters should wear some kind of head protection.

This heightened game play brought with it heightened stresses for the sane, rational, caring women who stood behind us, holding us up. Linda has always been very social, and hockey wives stick together, leaning on each other when the men aren't around. They brought their support to the games. To distract themselves from the intense game play and to keep from thinking about the physical risks their husbands were taking, the women would often talk shop, swapping recipes and the like during the games. We players were fortunate in many ways, indeed receiving some of the most delicious tried-and-true dishes around. Their stress was our gain, to be sure, and while we had diversified and upped our game on the ice, the European wives brought across the pond their expertise as well, including directions for creating some fantastic European dishes. Did I say win-win?

I remember once when they asked me if I would like to contribute a recipe to the growing cookbook. I said, "Sure. Here it is." They got ready with their pens and paper, and I continued. "Shoulder pads. Skates. Gloves. Tape. Mix them all together and you've got a good start to a winning combination."

As I am writing this chapter, it dawns on me that the WHA and Bobby Hull jumping ship and catapulting this new league into orbit was like a political movement in the United States, especially in relation to the 2016 presidential election. People were tired of the same old status-quo, the cronies, the establishment. Change was wanted. Accountability was wanted. Fairness. Recognition of the hard-working was wanted.

That was all going to be accomplished only by "draining the swamp," which the WHA did. What a revolution I experienced. Just as it is today, there are people on both sides of the fence, some who think the WHA was the answer, others who see it as a negative. Nevertheless, it undeniably changed the face of hockey.

It was in Winnipeg during the 1975-76 season that I received a letter, which I initially thought was fan mail and stuck in my cubicle to be opened when I had more time. I have always done my best to open every piece of fan mail I receive and respond whenever possible. About a month later, just before the crunch time of playoffs, I was going through the mail and opened the envelope, which was from Switzerland. I read the enclosed letter and saw that it was from the manager of a team in Switzerland. He said he had seen me play that game in Stockholm against the Swedish national team, that he had enjoyed my play, and that he wanted to talk to me about being a player/coach for a Swiss team. That was quite shocking, as I hadn't given serious consideration at that point to being a coach. I think most players at some point entertain the idea of coaching once they have decided (or someone has decided for them) that they are done playing, but I put those thoughts way back on a high shelf up to that point. Top shelf, though, it was. Given the timing, I set the letter aside until after the playoffs in Winnipeg. I didn't want anything to cloud my game play during the season. After winning the championship and reaching a monumental career goal, I telephoned the Swiss manager who had sent the letter and we agreed to meet. I could feel inside that the winds of change would once again be filling my sails.

Norm and Linda in their togas (1973)

Norm (left) and Aurel, after Aurel tried out for the Jets.

Norm with the Jets AVCO Cup

Jets ring (1976)

Chapter Six
_____

A NEW ADVENTURE IN HOCKEY

At the end of the 1975-76 season, I still had two years left on my contract with Winnipeg and things were going pretty well there, so I wasn't in any rush to leave. However, I suppose the years of practice we had in relocating stirred something inside, and I went to meet with the Swiss around June of 1976. They flew me to Bern, Switzerland, and the team was located in Langnau, about thirty kilometers, or a twenty-minute drive, from Bern. Langnau was a town of about 9,000 people, a great hockey town. The games would draw about 6,000 per game, it was a night out for everybody. What an enticing atmosphere for a hockey family!

The thought of leaving Winnipeg was both exciting and scary at the same time. It was tough because I was in my comfort zone, I had time left on my contract with a winning team, and I felt responsibilities not only toward Linda and my children, but also toward our whole community. Moving to Switzerland would deal us challenges in that we didn't speak German, and Langnau was a German town. Would it be a smart move to pack up four children and move them to a different continent into an area where they didn't even speak the language? Compelling me to make the change was the fact that I had been physically hurt more than I wanted to admit in those last couple of years. I had been hit in the head a couple of times, no helmet, you know, and I already had my eye on coaching somewhere in the future. (The good eye, that is, in case you were wondering.) The game at that time was still very rough, aggressive, and physical, so my body told me maybe it was time to give that up and move into a league that was not as aggressive. Another perk was that there would be much less traveling and only thirty to thirty-five games per year.

I did a lot of thinking on that plane ride home. The Langnau Tigers had presented me with a very good offer. When I returned to Winnipeg, it was time to discuss it with Linda, and surprisingly enough, she was up for a new adventure. I undoubtedly took it for granted at the time, but moving all over the place, several times a year, pregnant and with young ones had to have been an astronomically difficult task. The strength in Linda is nothing short of amazing. So, with her blessing, we signed the contracts. I told the Jets owners what I was doing, and I suppose they were shocked, but they understood that given my age, it was a good time to go. So, with a heavy heart, I left the team. We moved away from our home, our friends, our family, and we strode out on our new escapade.

Playing hockey had molded us for change. In Winnipeg, I had reached another pinnacle in my career. I played on a championship team. I felt I had been part of a great movement that was making hockey better for the world. With hockey, you are constantly striving to reach the next level, to win the next game, to up your stat's. Therefore, making a career move to another level seemed to be a sensible next step rather than staying in my current position.

On the day we arrived in Switzerland, we were exhausted. We had been on multiple flights, and then we drove to Langnau from Zurich. However, we were re-energized when we got into town and found out that the team had arranged a big spaghetti dinner for us, and most of the townsfolk were there. Wow—what a warm welcome!

The next morning, we woke up a big jet-lagged but rested (and hungry). We got dressed and walked to the nearest restaurant. We looked at the menu but couldn't read a thing on it, so I asked the waitress for bacon and eggs. I didn't speak German, and she didn't speak English or French. Uh-oh. Nothing on the menu must have sounded like "bacon and eggs," and I must have looked quite entertaining trying to mime out bacon and eggs. Finally, I just pointed at the bakery cabinet and put up six fingers indicating that we wanted food for six of us. The waitress seemed to understand perfectly, and satisfied that she finally understood what we wanted, I sat down and we waited for our breakfast. Shortly thereafter, Swiss Miss delivered six large slices of chocolate cake to our table. Although the kids seemed very impressed with my foreign food-ordering acumen and our new surroundings, the locals undoubtedly thought the Canadians were quite crazy, eating giant slabs of cake for breakfast. However, right after that, since we couldn't have the kids eating chocolate cake for breakfast every day, Linda and I spoke to the team management and told them that we needed to learn German—fast.

Another thing we learned early on, and fortunately, we had met a couple of people from the States who were able to give us some quick lessons on local customs and proprieties, is that you don't call someone by their first name, you had to address them as *Frau* Beaudin (lady) or *Herr* Beaudin (man), until you had been formally introduced and made a toast. It was more of a ritual actually, by linking arms and then drinking from your glass. Often you would also break bread at that time, and an old German tradition is to drink with the bread in the wine, which is where the word *toast* originates. After that point, you could call them by their first name. So, while Switzerland was more relaxed, it was also much more formal in ways. We would raise our glasses and say, "Prost."

We met many nice people there who had come from North America, including a nice lady who had come over from the United States to train as a dental hygienist. We met a man from Texas who we spent some time with. We met one woman, Frau Martine, whose son played hockey; she was very sweet and helped us learn the ways of living in Langnau. We had some other friends who gave me an extravagant gift for my birthday: a bunny. There we were in an apartment with four kids and a bunny hopping all over. It was no ordinary bunny; it was a fancy, pedigreed (probably very expensive) little guy that we kept as a pet. Having such wonderful people around us made it easy to assimilate into our new environment.

We did actually have some family in Switzerland, family that we hadn't met before. My sister Annette's husband, John, was from there, so he asked that we go to see his uncle, who was about twenty minutes from where we lived. It seems like everything was about twenty minutes from Langnau. One Sunday, we packed the family into the miniature Renault the team had given us (Europeans didn't drive big land yachts like we did in North America) and headed up into the mountains in the general direction they had told us to go. Along the way, still not speaking German, we kept asking people how to get to the Kaufman farm. We soon learned that *links* means left and *recht* means right. After more than a few stops and requests for directions, we finally found their place. It was a farm on a hill—a steep hill—and no one in the Renault wanted to ride up that steep hill to the farm in that itty-bitty car, so they all got out and walked up the hill while I drove. Thinking back, it probably wouldn't have made it up the hill with all of us in it, anyway.

We visited our newfound relatives for a few hours, and although we couldn't understand what they were speaking and they couldn't understand what we were saying, we pointed, shared pictures, pointed some more, and took a tour of their place. It was quite eye-opening to see people live so differently than we did. We saw those relatives from time to time after that. Their son would come visit us and watch some games, but he never learned to speak our language, and we didn't speak their dialect, so we always would just point. He would bring us chocolate. Quite possibly a perfect relationship.

The team that I would be working for, the Langnau Tigers, arranged everything to get us settled in. They found us a place to live, arranged for schooling for the kids, and provided us with a car—the whole deal. We were really starting to feel like grown-ups! The kids were to attend a diplomatic school, which would involve them taking the train to their school in another town about twenty minutes away. That was quite unsettling for us, putting our little five-year-old Carrie on a train, even though she was with her older siblings. They were in a strange new country full of people who talked differently, ate different foods (didn't everyone there eat chocolate cake for breakfast?), and even dressed differently. They, however, handled it like it wasn't any big deal at all. Kids are so adaptable and resilient. At least ours were. We would take them to the train in the morning, and when the school day was over, they were escorted to the train station, they got back on the train, and we picked them up at the depot that was right next to our apartment.

At times, that whole feeling-like-a-grown-up thing was put in its place, however, especially when we went to the grocery store. In North America, you go to the grocery store, pick up the produce, give the tomatoes a gentle squeeze, look at them on all sides, put back the ones you don't like, and go on until you have chosen the best of the stack to buy. Employing this method, we soon found ourselves being given slight smacks on the back of the hand and even being yelled at completely unintelligibly. We quickly learned that in Europe, it is not polite to touch produce that you do not purchase. How could we have known? Okay, so we picked out our groceries, and with no carts in sight, piled the kids' arms high with a week's worth of food, walked past the gawking strangers, and piled it all on the counter. Only there were no bags at the counter. You're supposed to bring your own? Somehow, we completed the transaction, loaded the kids up again with food—arms full of loose groceries, dropping apples along the way—and walked to the car with our bounty, heads held high. We were definitely the talk of the town for a while, the entertainment. When we got back to our apartment, we discovered why people shop every day or every other day. The refrigerators are tiny. I mean tinier than tiny—tiny like in a hotel room tiny, not week's-worth-of-food-for-six size. Ah. See how much we were learning on this adventure? I think the kids started thinking that their parents were just giant dumb-dumbs, but fortunately for us all, we had plenty of practice at thinking and adapting quickly.

Some other people that we met and became friends with early on had a son who played hockey with our son Dave, and they invited us to their home to play cards. On our first visit there, we realized it's easy enough to count and figure out how to win, even with a language barrier, so we ended up learning a great deal of German with them over the years by just playing cards. On our first visit, we learned something new and of great value. Many of the more rural homes had the barn attached to the house. We had been playing cards for a while when Linda asked to use the washroom. They pointed toward the barn, and Linda thought, no, and pointed up the stairs, saying the German word for washroom. Again, they pointed to the door off the kitchen where they had shown us the attached barn. The lady of the house walked Linda through the door and out to the lavatory, which was indeed in the barn, along with the pigs, the cows, and whatever other animals they were raising. Even a greater surprise was that it did not have a door. So, there was Linda, using the facilities with giant furry faces and big curious eyes on either side of her. After that, you knew to use the lavatory at home before game night and not to drink much while you were playing cards there.

Hockey had prepared our family for challenges, and in this case, there were obvious challenges, challenges galore. We missed our friends. We missed our family. We didn't make any trips home for three years. However, in true Beaudin fashion, we all rose to the challenge. Coaching was another uphill battle, but the hockey was good. It was very fast hockey but not too aggressive, and you didn't have the nagging fear that you might get killed by somebody.

Throughout Switzerland, there are different dialects of German, as well as other languages spoken, so for my first year coaching and playing, I spoke through an interpreter. I would speak French to him, and he would relay in German what I wanted done. As soon as we could, Linda and I went to school every weekday for two months to learn German, so my second year I was teaching in German. Linda and I had learned high German, but the locals and most of the team spoke a dialect that I didn't understand. It was difficult, and I couldn't understand them, but they understood me, and not only did we make it work, it was fun. We made great friends—hockey friends and friends outside of the hockey world.

One of our new friends was the parent of a player who owned a local butcher shop, where we started buying our meat. We wanted to support the locals and the people we knew, so on our first visit, we pointed and ordered a little of this, a little of that. Not too much, because tiny fridge, remember? That night Linda had cooked some meat, and the kids were eating slowly, finally asking what they were eating. It wasn't bad, but different. I liked it. Since the kids were not satisfied with our answer of "meat," the next day I asked the butcher what meat we had purchased, and he eventually got across to me that it was horse meat, commonly served there. Hmm. That was a tough one to share with the kids. After that, they told us in no uncertain terms that they would be eating no more horse meat.

At school, the kids took classes to learn German and French, and soon they were able to communicate with their local friends. This move opened up our world so much. The kids developed a large circle of friends—an elite one—and in turn, introduced many of them to the world of hockey. Having them around helped Linda and I learn the language as well, except for Carrie who was only five and didn't have many friends outside of the house. Most importantly, when I made my speeches before the games, the players understood what I said, but a couple of times I had to remind them, whatever you do, don't laugh at me, don't laugh at the way I speak on the ice. If you want to laugh about it, do it in the bar afterward that's fine. They had a few laughs at my expense, but it was very satisfying to be speaking German on the ice, even if it was Beaudin German.

I remember one game in which Langnau was playing Bern (in Bern), another sold-out game, with seventeen or eighteen thousand people watching. There the crowd stands up for the whole game. They stand and sing; it's quite the affair. Bern was a rival, so we went into this important game really wanting to win. In addition, the Embassy people were there and had a big party scheduled for us afterward. I told my players, "No stupid penalties. We can't afford penalties."

We couldn't afford any penalties because Bern had a very good team; they were going to be tough to beat. I gave my pre-game speech in German and was confident if we played well, we could win that game in front of my friends. There was a lot of pressure on that night, so I started in the game. I was forechecking, setting a good pace, there we go, and I gave a shot to this guy in the corner. He turned and said, "You f*n Canadian, you…" He hit too many buttons with that comment, and something clicked inside me, this normally composed number 17. I just drilled that jerk in the face. I hit him hard and ended up with a five-minute major. There I had just told my team, "No stupid penalties," and I was the first one sitting in the penalty box. That was five of the longest minutes of my career, and I was the coach. But I felt I was defending not only my team, but also my country.

Linda had seen it all, and boy was she mad. She had to take the brunt of the criticism from the other wives and our friends after I had told her I would have a nice, calm game in front of them, and I went out and did that. There was even another European ambassador that was there staying with our embassy friends—what an embarrassment! After the game, Linda came up to me and asked me what was up. What did that man do to make me hit him like that? I told her he called me an f*n Canadian, and she said, "Well, why didn't you hit him again?" Always my defensive little spitfire, that Linda.

Anyway, I got the five-minute major, but the team held on and even scored so then we were up one to zero. It turned out positive, my move was quite the motivator, and we won that game. The Embassy people still welcomed us in and had a dance for us that night. However, the newspaper headlines the next day said, "Beaudin Schwarze Schafe" meaning "Beaudin Black Sheep," and yep, that stuck.

In the two seasons that I had with the Langnau Tigers, I think we only lost thirteen games. I played right wing, and I had a couple of good centers. We had a good team, a really good team. We were actually the elite team of the league that first year. In my second year, we lost six games. In Europe, in that league, if you end up first in your division, you've won the championship. There aren't any playoffs, and the first year, we were one point behind, and the second year, if we won the last game, we would have been champions. Did we win? No, and the reason we lost was that management had set up a game against the Czechs and told our goalie to play. He ended up getting sick and did not play another game. We were forced to use our backup goalie. That cost us the championship, and along with my ongoing theme, it cost me a lot of money. It was a tough pill to take because we were so close.

That was definitely the hardest part, for me personally, of being in Switzerland. It was game-related. Switzerland itself was wonderful. To this day, Linda remembers and reminisces about the ambience. It was like going back in time to a more peaceful and a simpler way of life. Just nice. Really nice, she says. We would spend time with our diplomatic friends every Sunday after church. We would get together and watch videotaped movies, as we had to watch them in English because we didn't understand the movies in the theater. The people at the embassy were so good to us. We would go to the commissary in Germany, and we could get liquor, food, anything. It was such a treat. Life was great there. One time, we went to the theater to watch the movie *Slap Shot* with Paul Newman and the Hanson brothers. It was in English with German subtitles and we thought it was hilarious, but we were the only ones laughing. Obviously, the translation must not have been too funny, but we sure laughed. Maybe it was extra funny because we knew some of the guys in the movie. It certainly brought us a bit of home that day and probably even made us a little homesick.

We had a great time while we were in Switzerland, but life with children is never without incidents and tragedies. I recall one time when Linda and I had gone up into the mountains, it was near Christmas-time and the kids were at home. The boys were having a boy scouting meeting, and we had just sat down at a dinner table, overlooking the beautiful vista. Suddenly, the peace was interrupted by a telephone ring and then screaming coming from the handset. Apparently, the boys had decided to cook hotdogs, and when they tried to drain the pot, Carrie, always wanting to be involved, got really involved and somehow got the boiling water poured all over her hands. All we could hear was her screaming, it was terrible. We grabbed our coats and flew down the hill and got her to the hospital. The mother of one of the boys' friends was a nurse at the hospital, and she certainly helped calm us down. The Christmas presents weren't the only things wrapped up that year. Poor little Carrie couldn't even open a gift with her hands all bandaged up.

That wasn't the only scary story about Carrie. One day, instead of coming home, Greg asked if he could spend the night with one of his buddies from the embassy group. We agreed, as long as he would put Carrie on the train first. Well, young boys being young boys, they apparently decided that getting her to the train station would be good enough. They put her on a bench and went about their merry way. It turns out that day we had a man in from Winnipeg who was talking to us about contracts and possible future ventures. We were holding the business meeting at home. At about the right time, we went to the train station, and when Carrie didn't get off the train the madness started. We were panicked. Everyone had always been so good about looking after the kids; it was part of the deal that the conductors would watch over the kids while they were on the train; we couldn't imagine where she was. There were no cell phones back then, so we had to use the land line, and people were calling everywhere trying to find Carrie. Finally, she was located. On the bench where the boys had left her. She hadn't even got on a train. Someone had given her an ice cream cone, and she was perfectly content to just eat that cone and watch the trains go by. Those concerned train employees were so kind, one of them got on the train and rode with her all the way home. That day, she got ice cream and a lot of attention; we got a few more gray hairs.

Speaking of gray hairs, hockey was to provide me with another bumper crop of those as well. We had such a good team there in Langnau and it was such a good hockey town. We saw great success but not a championship during my tenure. Even if you perform well, if you don't win the championship, something changes. I had a three-year contract with the Tigers, but after that second year, the team in Sierre, Switzerland, the French part across the mountains, was looking for a coach. They had quite a bad season and needed a new leader, so the owner of the Tigers asked if I would mind moving over to a different town. I couldn't rightfully say no, so off we went, to Sierre, another spectacularly beautiful area laced with vineyards. This would be another challenge for the family, uprooting the kids and moving them to another area. I spoke French, but I had never taught the kids, and the kids had focused on learning their German over the last two years. The wheels had already been put in motion and the teams were in agreement, so we negotiated a new contract with the French team in Sierre, in the Valais.

Hockey wasn't the only thing we did while we were in Europe. With the long off-season, we were able to travel all summer. We had six months off, and we went to France, Germany, Austria, and Italy. One summer, we all squished into the Renault, and I drove the family to Italy. We had made reservations to stay at an exclusive place on the Ligurian Sea on the west side of Italy, and we drove for a couple of days to get there, which was a real treat. You can imagine all of us packed into that car like a tin of sardines, four kids in the back, driving for two days. Finally we arrived in gorgeous Punta Ala, and we're not looking so gorgeous. The resort was absolutely spectacular, although it did have the aura of a mafia presence, which we had been warned about. We pulled into the portico out front, went in to register, and were told they didn't have a room for us. What? We had fully paid reservations before we left! I pressed the issue, and all of a sudden, they found our reservation, but we would be going to stay a ways away from the beach at a property on the hillside. It seemed to have been a set-up. The check-in clerk looked at me and asked if we brought a bed. Was she crazy? Where in that car would we have a bed? I said, "Do you see a f'n bed on my back?" I guess she got the idea that I wasn't going away, so they put us up in a real nice chalet with enough beds for all of us. It felt good to finally settle in, get the kids to bed, fill a glass with good wine, and clink my glass to Linda's with a thankful "saluti."

That Sunday we went to church, and from the look of it, it was an area heavily influenced by the mafia. It all seemed very blatant. You could just see it, feel it. Nevertheless, it was beautiful and peaceful, and we had a great time. We spent a couple of weeks there, explored the areas, ate delicious food, and showed the kids a great time.

On one occasion, we arranged to meet friends in Paris, France. They said they knew of a good restaurant, I can't recall the name, but as we were sitting there eating, suddenly there was a lamb walking around—a lamb just strutting around, visiting tables, getting petted here, getting treats there. I'm not sure if he was on the menu or was rescued from the menu or what, but the food was good. Bon appetit!

Another off-ice story with the kids, oh, those kids: it was ski season, and Dave and Greg had joined the Boy Scout program. Most of the kids were diplomat kids, not local Germans. Somehow, I was appointed to be a chaperone, and we went to the mountains for the weekend. I was in charge of ski patrol; I guess they thought because I could ice skate that I would be a good snow skier. That's not quite how it works, but I went along. We took off to ski, and I was overseeing about ten kids when, all of a sudden, I see a big sign that says "**Caution: Avalanche Area, Do Not Enter.**" What do those boys do but head straight past that sign! I'm back there yelling—remember I'm not a good skier—I can't quite keep up with them. We're in Switzerland, where kids ski all the time, and they just took off with me following behind them, yelling at them to stop. What do they do? They go right in. I wonder what the hell to do, and I realize *I have to follow them in.* I have faced some perilous situations at times, but that was one of the scariest. After the seemingly endless trek, we made it through, and I emerged from the other side with knuckles whiter than the whitest snow we had trudged through and an even stronger desire to stay on the ice and *never* ski again—which I didn't.

I survived the Alps, and come August, it was back to training camp, this time with Sierre, and things were looking good. We had a good team and training camp, so I'm like a king there. We started the season going into Bern, where it is very tough to play. They draw large crowds of around 18,000 people, and we went in and beat them in their own house. We came home and won our second game, our third game, and then our fourth. Now, we're hot—really hot. I'm looking at maybe a championship team. We were four and zero. In that league, we played one game a week. There were thirty games on the schedule, which was an easy schedule, and we would have three practices per week. That made for a nice life.

We were on a four-straight win streak, hadn't lost a game, so the team higher-ups told me there was a guy named Jacque Plante living up in the mountains whom they thought I may like as my assistant. Well, for sure, I thought. Jacque had been in the NHL for seventeen or eighteen years or so, eventually becoming a hall-of-famer, and I had played with him in St. Louis and Montreal. He hadn't been at training camp, but he came later to help out, so I told him to go take care of the defensemen. He came into the picture a few games into the season, and we kept rolling. During the next game, we lost a couple of players to injuries, and we didn't win. The next game, we lost another player. Those injured were all of my top players. We couldn't win a game after that. We ended up losing six regulars to injuries, some off-ice. I lost three defensemen: one had a brain aneurysm, one had a car accident, and one had a dislocated shoulder. Just freak accidents. The guy with the aneurysm was my toughest guy. The guy in the car accident, he was tough, a big, strong kid. The other guy was an all-star with the Swiss National Team. All of this happened within a few games. Then, I lost my best centerman goal scorer. I lost my Canadian, another top scorer, and I lost my other centerman. I was left with only one center, which meant I had to play, but we still couldn't win a game. We were decimated to say the least. Even though I knew that I didn't fail the team, it didn't make me feel any better; injuries had just killed us. I was devastated.

As far as Jacque, we parted ways since there was no use keeping him. I got rid of another guy on the bench, and there was just so much turmoil. We lost thirteen games—couldn't win—and although it seemed like we lost by only one goal every game, we just didn't have the horses to get another win. We finished with a losing season. While I felt I had failed at my job, away from the rink, it was offset by the beauty of Sierre and with the nice people there. The culture there was very fun-loving, less strict than Langnau, but we just couldn't get the job done that we were there to do. I didn't think the team would keep me on, but about a week before we were set to leave, they offered me a new contract. It was a good contract, which included housing and a car. I agreed, as it sounded too good to pass up. With that contract in the books, we left for a summer in Winnipeg. They told me to find a good Canadian player and bring him back with me to fill out the team, and that he could be a player/coach if I felt that would be a good fit. Little did I know I had just taken off my Siders jersey for the last time.

March 4, 1979 brought us back to Winnipeg. I immediately set out to evaluate players and find someone I could take back to Switzerland with me. I had several in mind and was getting ready to return to Europe when I opened a Winnipeg Free Press paper and saw an article stating that Jacque Lemaire had signed with the Sierre club as the coach. Wait, what? That was my job! Things went there as they tend to go in professional sports from time to time. I, still doing things my way, with no agent, called them, and we came to an agreement. My contract was bought out, and they went with Lemaire as coach. Crazy, right? I read about it in a Canadian newspaper? Interesting that I was replaced by a Hall of Famer, which was actually an honor.

So, that is how my time in Europe came to an end. I got my walking papers from a Canadian newspaper, but in the big picture, it was time to go home. The kids were ready to go back to Canada, back to our family and the good friends we had been missing so much. Throughout our years, we really didn't take the attitude that we were leaving somewhere, but rather that we were going somewhere. While it was a goodbye, it was a welcome hello and excitement all over again.

Norm working on a farm in Switzerland (1977)

Norm, Langnau Tigers player/coach (1976)

Chapter Seven

BACK TO THE HOMELAND

Luckily, even though hockey is a sport, it prepared me for life after the game—for life in general, really. I am always ready for a challenge, always ready to be thrown into a new situation, face a new culture, a new language, a new business. Hockey taught me to always think on my feet, to deal with a variety of unpredictable situations and temperaments, and to make calls at a moment's notice, all while staying calm. After preparation like that, life off the ice should be a breeze, right? Well it is, and it isn't.

The whole Switzerland and Europe situation was incredible, invaluable. The kids learned German and French, experienced different cultures, firsthand, and got to spend weeks at a time in beautiful places like France, Austria, and Italy. We got closer as a family, and the kids got closer to each other. Literally closer, given the size of the car we had. Look at the little Fiats on the road today, and you'll see what we rolled around in, all six of us. Two adults, four kids, and all the gear. I don't know how we did it, but after three years, we were ready for it to come to an end. We were ready to return to Winnipeg. It felt so good to get back home and reestablish ourselves there. We even went back to the same house, and it felt so good.

There were things that were difficult about returning home. Of course, the kids missed their European friends at first, and they missed skiing. They had put down some fairly deep roots over the three years that we were in Switzerland. For me, the hardest part about leaving was not so much what I was leaving but what I was going *to*: uncertainty. Never in my life had I faced a future off the ice. I would have to establish myself in a new world, and I really wasn't ready to leave hockey. At times, I felt as though I should have stayed in the game, that I shouldn't have left Winnipeg early, but a happy life involves not having regrets, so I did my best to stay positive and focused, looking to the future.

It was nice to return to our good, stable neighborhood in Winnipeg. We were members of a nice country club, and we had very good friends there. Linda was very happy to be back in Canada but in ways missed Switzerland. She missed the food, the people, the small community, and the low crime rate. It was hard to leave the friends that we had there, our surrogate family. We left behind a lifestyle, and it was a lifestyle that had been happily sewn into the fabric of our family.

Considering how crazy things went with the Swiss contract debacle, I thought I was ready to retire from playing hockey professionally. I probably wasn't, but as was usual, hockey dictated life instead of me dictating life, so when hockey wasn't there, I floundered a bit. However, I needed to go to work. It was probably in July 1979 or so, after getting settled in and finding out that we would not be returning to Switzerland, that I got my resumé together. I never had to do that before. What a strange document, to have to tout your skills and abilities on paper to people who don't know anything about you. No film, no training camp, no slap shot to whiz past an out-of-practice goalie. Just a flimsy piece of paper.

I started handing out resumés to all my friends and connections, passing them out like candy on Halloween, but I didn't know the protocol. Ultimately, it wasn't a resumé, but a personal contact that got me an interview with someone in the liquor industry. Being in hockey, I did have an exaggerated level of exposure to liquor, that's for sure.

The liquor industry in Canada is quite different from that in Europe or the United States. It is all highly regulated by the government, and the stores are not privately owned. Therefore, you have to train to work in that field; you've got to know what you're doing. Sound familiar? Like another challenge? While I knew what liquor looked and tasted like, I didn't know anything about marketing or selling it. Buddy Tinsley, who played football for the Winnipeg Blue Bombers, was in the industry and became a rep for a company called Melchers, and through his recommendation, I got the job as his assistant.

You couldn't beat the job because we had all the liqueurs; we had hard stuff; we had beer—everything. We had wines, nice wines. Once I was formally hired, I went to a meeting, and they trained me to go about my job in accordance with all the requirements. There were about maybe thirty stores in Manitoba. In Winnipeg, just the city alone, there were quite a few, so I had a big job.

So, there I was, hired to work for Melchers Distillery, which was a subsidiary of Corby: a private company that dealt with the government. My job was to go to different stores and make sure our product was displayed properly, to see how it was selling, and so forth. I can't remember my title, but it wasn't right wing. I guess it's not related to hockey, so it just didn't stick in the mind.

People outside of Canada may be surprised at how some of the liquor business works there, so let me go into a bit more detail. Another part of my job was making recommendations for weddings and socials, to let the customers know how much liquor they could use, fill out the permit application, bring it to the government, and have them sign off on it. I don't know if it's still that way today, but back then in Canada, you had to have a permit for any event that allowed liquor, and there were limits per person as to how much alcohol you could have at an event. I would work with them to pair their alcohols with their menu items, make suggestions and recommendations, and close the deals. If you overdid it and asked for too much alcohol, the government would veto the permit. If they showed up and you had too much alcohol in comparison to the number of people in your party, they would take the liquor away. Perfectly good alcohol gone bye-bye. The government would allot the alcohol, the beer, and the wine, and it had to be clearly marked on the permit, which I would fill out. I would take the approved permit to the customer and have the commission deliver the products, or I could pick them up and deliver them myself. As you can surmise, there were definitely occasions for which I enjoyed making the deliveries personally.

Another facet of my job was to visit restaurants and make wine recommendations. I would try to get the wine on their menus or wine lists as a regular item, which was good for business. People would ask for the products by name, and they would return if they enjoyed them or purchase the products at a different establishment.

Another responsibility of my job included taking clients out golfing, and we would try to promote our liquor and wines, so it was a perfect job. They gave me a car and paid me well. The job wasn't strenuous; it was like a great social time for me. I was like a sales rep; every week I would send my expense report into the company in Montreal, and they would send me a check back for all that along with my paycheck. I was with them for about a year and a half, and then I must have got the itch to move again and did something crazy. I know you probably find it hard to believe that I would do something unusual and crazy, but yes, that's precisely what I did.

My brother-in-law was in the Quonset-hut selling business, peddling them all over Saskatchewan and greater Canada, and he needed help meeting the demands of his job, so he talked me into working with him. What was I thinking? There we were, selling huts to farmers, anyone whom we could talk into purchasing one. Hearing all the talk about big money and, of course, me being ready for an almost regularly-scheduled change (only this time it was more of an experiment), I quit the job that I loved and jumped headfirst into this new venture—a venture I, of course, knew nothing about.

I should have made sure to iron out the details before I agreed to jump into that pond, but I didn't, and right away they told me they wanted me to move to Saskatoon and work from there. Moving has never been an obstacle for me, so I agreed. I worked there for about a month, and then Linda came down and picked out a beautiful home for us. It was priced very well so we put $10,000 down on it, even though we were apprehensive to do so because we hadn't yet sold our home in Winnipeg and interest rates at that time were through the roof, pun intended. They were somewhere in the ballpark of twenty percent, crazy enough. Sometimes it seems like someone from beyond is looking out for us, because right after that, the new job fell through, and we had to go back to Winnipeg. We ended up giving up the deposit on that house, but it was better to do that than have a home we didn't need, so we moved back, and I was once again in the job market.

There we were, back in Winnipeg, only this time I decided to try something different. I decided to apply for a job that I already knew how to do. Having kids makes one crazy like that, I suppose. This time, though, through a good friend, Ted Foreman, I got a job with Meagher's Distillers. Ted was our financial guy, a great guy, and he recommended me to the manager of the company. Because I did have recent, relevant experience, they hired me right away. It was a good company, we had great products: a full line of liquor, liqueurs, and wines. Wines from France, Italy, Spain, South Africa—you name it, we had it.

I represented all our products and loved my work. Just like hockey, it wasn't a job; it was a *great job*. I was with them for about seven years and during that time we had many good parties and events, and we even toured Europe with the company. They took Linda and me to the vineyards of France, where wonderful wines such as Bordeaux, Bourgogne, and Burgundy are produced. We visited several vineyards there, and it was the best of all worlds. Then we went to Paris for a week because we represented multiple French products. They took us to shows in Montmartre, which was special to me because that was the same name as the small town in which I was born and raised.

After Paris, we went to Italy where we visited the regions of Chianti and Ruffino. They took us to Milan and gave us the royal-grand tour, that's for sure. Talk about an experience. We were in Europe for three weeks, toured all over the place, went for helicopter rides, saw the beautiful green hills where Dom Perignon and Cognac come from. It was another stellar time on the European continent.

I was certainly having a fantastic time at my new career, but I hadn't left the old one behind, to be certain. About the longest time I had been off of the ice was around a year, right after I got back from Switzerland. It should have been a momentous occasion to get back on the ice, but I think it was just like being back home, like I *should* be there, so I just picked right up where I had left off—no special fanfare.

I started playing hockey with the Oldtimers and the Manitoba Clubs. Club is a beer, which is a Labatt's Blue product. Aptly, we were called the Winnipeg Clubs.

Can you see how well my two careers merged? A perfect marriage. I would play about once a week, and I played in quite a lot of tournaments.

On one hockey trip, we happened to be in Germany for New Year's Eve. We were in Munich and a group of us were having a late dinner at a nice restaurant. We ate and ate, and we drank and drank. Oh, it reminds me that we were young at one time. Well, one of the guys was having fun, a lot of fun, and decided that he needed to get on top of a table and do a strip-tease for anyone who would watch. He turned heads, that's for sure. I don't know how long it took for them to get all of us out of there, but eventually we made our way back to the hotel to rest up for the next stop.

I also played with the Winnipeg Jets alumni. We would play in many different towns in Manitoba, also playing in charity games to raise funds for hockey programs in many different arenas. It felt really good to help get those programs going and thriving. We have seen a lot of great hockey players come out of Manitoba, so the interest is there; sometimes the funding for gear and travel is the only thing holding those kids back, and we were able to fill that gap.

The teams that I worked with, the people in the community, and the people at Meaghers Distillers—we all had great camaraderie. It was a perfect union to blend my hockey world with my sales world. The customers were fantastic and everything worked so well together. In addition, the travel was quite a benefit.

I also traveled a great deal with my post-pro hockey teams, both domestically and abroad. I went back to Europe with the Montreal Oldtimers for a third time with a new group, not the guys with whom I had regularly played. There were a few guys from Winnipeg, but most of them were drawn from other areas. We went to Austria, Germany, France, and Switzerland. The game in Austria was crazy. It was an exhibition game, and Rocket Richard, arguably the best player in the world at the time, was a referee, and his brother was playing. We ended up scoring twenty goals, just an absolute blowout. When we played in Switzerland, we played the Swiss National team—that was an extra-special part of the trip because I knew a lot of the players and personnel there.

Working for Meaghers, I represented some French wines, and after we played in Strasbourg, we were going through the Alsace area—the wine country of France. I knew some people at a vineyard there, so I suggested we make a little unscheduled visit. Visit we did. All thirty of us. Thirty hockey players walked into that vineyard led by me. One of our players was the infamous Eddie Shack, known for the chant in a song "Clear the track, here comes Shack." He was an old-school hockey guy, a genuine tough guy that was, I'll just say, rough around the edges. So, there we were, having lunch and sampling wines at this fancy vineyard in France and Shack—of all guys—was the most knowledgeable about the wines. I mean he knew his stuff, and before we left, he ordered twelve cases of his favorite one shipped to Canada.

Before we hit the road in the bus, the vineyard stocked us up well with wine, which in hindsight was not only *not* a good idea, but a very bad idea. Traveling after a boozy lunch on a bus with more wine on windy roads is not a good combination. We had to ride in that stuffy bus back to Zurich and get right on a plane. Some of the guys really didn't look like they wanted to get on our flight. I'm not a guy who drinks much, but I felt responsible for getting those guys drunk and sick, and I can say with conviction that was not one of my better achievements. However, they were big boys, and no one held them down and poured the wine into their mouths, that's for sure. Regardless, it was nice being able to stop there and to not only introduce my hockey friends to people I knew, but also show them some of what I did off the ice—even if they didn't remember all of it. That was in 1984.

1984 was a good year—one of those years that stands out to me. I was back home and playing hockey; the kids at that point were doing great; Carrie and Greg were going to school; Nadine was working at a restaurant and going to high school; and Dave went to Ohio State on a hockey scholarship. I was one proud poppa.

I was, however, not involved much in the kids' hockey. I coached a bit but was not involved in depth. They had their teams and coaches, and I didn't want to be one of those over-bearing parents whom everyone cringes away from. I just wanted to watch them play and have fun. Dave had developed his game in Switzerland. He had super skills that he had learned there. Unfortunately, he got hurt pretty badly too many times, so he didn't end up going pro, but it was fun while it lasted. He is still involved in the field, and his son is excelling on the ice.

One year, one of my fellow hockey players, George Smith, a Russian guy who had Jets season tickets and owned a big trucking company, decided our team should go to Russia. He volunteered to pick up the tab, so just before Christmas, we went to Russia for ten days to play hockey. We went there with what we thought was an average team—I think I was the only pro there. The other guys played senior hockey; they were old guys, heavy guys, but good hockey players.

We went to Moscow; they had set up three games for us to play. We showed up to a sold-out house of about 15,000 spectators, and who walked out of the locker room? Their elite team: the Russian National Team, the Red Army! Up against that, saying that we did not do great is an understatement. They were good. Man, were they good. They were all young, tough, and in shape. Half our guys weren't in shape. Well, round is a shape, but it's not hockey-shape, so basically, we got our stick-whipped and puck-burned butts handed to us by those Russians. We had a couple of defensemen who were 250, even 300 pounds. We looked like a bunch of idiots out there. We had a couple of good lines, but they beat the you-know-what out of us. They had invited us, so we went, and we got to play hockey in a new country. Nothing wrong with that.

There were some things wrong with that trip, though, let me tell you.

We walked off the plane and into trouble. As we were gathering our gear, the Russians in charge told us that we couldn't leave the airport until we paid them five thousand dollars! That's how things worked there at that time, that was one of the tactics they used on foreigners, basically holding your belongings for ransom. I don't know how it is now, but I won't be finding out in person, no way, no how. There we were, stuck. None of us had the five grand we wanted to give to those gangsters. We also weren't about to leave without our gear. Eventually, one of our guys was able to call the hockey federation and explain to them what was going on, that we were playing their team, and one of the representatives from there, I think his name was Federov, came to the airport and ironed things out. We left without paying a dime and went straight to the hotel, hoping that was the end of the drama. It wasn't.

Getting around was very difficult, and traveling on the underground trains was nothing short of a crap-shoot. Unlike most European countries, most of the Russians there did not speak English. If you didn't speak Russian, you were out of luck, and you didn't know where you would end up. Fortunately, the guy Smith who had taken us there and paid for everything hung around with us most of the time and did the interpreting for us. I still wonder how on Earth we didn't lose someone.

The food in Moscow was quite different than that to which we were accustomed. We ate a lot of cold food: borscht, cold cuts, edible foods, but not like home. Everything seemed to be cold except for the beer, which should have been cold. The Russians had western beer available for us, but they served it warm, like European beer, and it tasted terrible, because it is not crafted to be served at room temperature. Being a liquor salesman, this really got under my skin.

Eventually, despite the language barrier, we got across to them that we wanted our beer chilled, and we were self-satisfied to have culturally enriched them. At least I was. Still on the job, I guess. They would also vend beer from an "American" kiosk. I remember having Heineken there, but it was always warm. On that trip, nothing was consistent or customary or predictable.

After the game, we all went together—both teams, all the players, and the Russian dignitaries—to a big get-together with dinner and drinks. There with the Russians sat our team, a bunch of beer-drinkers, celebrating and drinking vodka, because we just couldn't palate that warm beer. Toast after toast, we'd drink to this, we'd drink to that, the vodka was going down like water. Only it wasn't water. About two hours later, half of our team was laid out, couldn't even walk. They all had to take cabs or whatever back to the hotel because they couldn't even stand up. The Russians? They were fine. They were used to drinking vodka, so they beat us on and off the ice.

I also realized something else on that trip. One would swirl the liquid in their glass, give a good look, give it a sniff, then *heartily* raise their glass to toast. Budem

Zdorovo! The key here is in "heartily" or perhaps more accurately, *rigorously*. Give your fellow drinkers a firm tap with your glass and *voila!* A skilled drinker can toss maybe half of their drink into the other glass, leaving only about half a shot to consume, while the other party is drinking a shot and a half. Even if you aren't able to slosh part of your drink into their glass, worst case, it will go out of your glass onto their hand, glove, and sleeve. Just don't stand too close when they go to light their cigar.

We also had to learn about the local currency, and I'm not talking about rubles. In Russia, pantyhose was the currency of choice for many a transaction. Seriously! Pantyhose! Fortunately, we had been tipped off to this prior to our trip, so we stuffed the empty corners of our bags with nylon women's stockings before we left Canada. I'm not sure if everyone did, some of us certainly wondered if someone was pulling a fast one on us, especially when we got tied up at the airport when we arrived, but it turned out to be a hot tip.

Trade and commerce in Russia were quite different than they were in Europe, Canada, or the United States. There seemed to be gestapos on every corner, and as we walked down the street, people would quietly call out to us from doorways and between buildings. They would peddle their wares from nooks and crannies you couldn't even see. They even called out from behind curtains in the hotel lobby, and they would usher us down a hallway where they could make their sales pitches to us.

We couldn't say no; we were afraid to say no, so we would duck into their corners, and they would show us what they were selling—everything you can think of from food to clothing to toys and so much more. They would trade for the pantyhose! Apparently, pantyhose were not readily available there, and they could really score big with their women in that cold country if they brought home new stockings. Or maybe they wore the pantyhose themselves, who knows. They would also trade for other items you had with you, but you had to make the deal go down without attracting the attention of the gestapos. You really didn't feel like you could say no to these people, so the transactions were made. I traded for things like sets of matryoshka dolls (nesting dolls) for my kids and fine crystal for Linda and the relatives back home.

I mentioned that the trip was right before Christmas, and I was scheduled to be home before the rest of the team. The liquor company and my family said I had to be back by Christmas, so three days before Christmas, I told the front desk personnel at the hotel that I wanted a cab there at four o'clock the next morning to take me to the airport, giving me time to make the long journey home.

Early that morning on the 23rd, I think it was 1987, there I was, all alone in this Russian cab heading toward the airport—or so I thought. The driver spoke no English and barely glanced at me as we began our drive. I believed he was clear in understanding that I needed to make it to the airport to catch a flight home. We rode along in silence, and all of a sudden, as quick as a thirsty Russian centerman downs his celebratory shot after a big win, the driver makes a series of quick turns, and we're driving down into what I can best describe as a dark basement. No explanation, nothing, just driving and driving and driving down this dark, musty, underground passageway, toward the gates of hell.

The air was thick with the smell of things like tires, exhaust, smoke, and mildew. I've smelled hockey bags that smelled much better. I thought for sure I was not going to make it out of that dungeon alive. My gear was in the trunk, I had nothing to hit the guy with, and I figured he probably had a gun anyway, so what good would my stick do against a spray of bullets. So, I just rode along, trying to see into the darkness and plan what I would do. Just as quickly as he had veered off of the main route, the guys stops, parks, gets out of the car, and what? Fills it up with gas! He must have had some area where he could get black market petrol down there, and that's what he did, without a word. He finished filling up, got back in the car, drove straight out of that netherworld and to the airport in silence.

I was so happy to survive that excursion that when we got to the airport, I gave the driver a gift in the form of a Jets banner that I highly prized and had wanted to bring home. That was one of the scariest moments of my life, feeling so helpless down there in the dark. That was all of Russia I will ever see. I went back to Europe later to play with the Oldtimers, but not back to Russia—no way. I'm done there.

It felt so good to make it home from that trip that I had a renewed energy I directed toward charitable ventures. Another benefit that was provided to us during my time in Winnipeg was the opportunity to assist in church activities, and I poured as much time as possible into them. I was instrumental in organizing a hockey game to benefit the Catholic schools in the area. I brought the Jets' older players or alumni players, which included Bobby Hull, AB McDonald, Joe Daley, and my old centerman Christian Bordeleau, reuniting the Luxury Line. In conjunction with the Knights of Columbus, we were fortunate to bring in the Flying Fathers to play on the other side of the puck. The Flying Fathers were Catholic priests who traveled around North America, playing hockey and raising money to help young people and the unfortunate. Their motto was, "We skate to beat hell," and it showed!

I remember having something like 12,500 people purchase tickets to the game to help the cause, so it was a very successful organized hockey game that benefited a lot of people. I take great satisfaction in knowing that I was able to organize the event. I carry with me many fond memories of my time in Winnipeg, and all the wonderful people that I knew and met there.

One crazy charitable move I made was on a Father's Day after I had returned from Switzerland. I was challenged at the last minute to run a marathon by friends of ours, Gary and Joanne. They sponsored me, and they did so for a good sum of money, so I agreed to run the marathon. I had zero training, so Gary figured I would run for five miles, which didn't sound too far off the mark. The most I had ever run at one time was two miles, and right before the marathon, I tested things out and ran just over two miles. Nevertheless, I decided I was up for the challenge.

I knew what worked for me as far as hockey pre-game preparation, but I was just taking shots in the dark with a marathon. Hockey games didn't start early in the morning. For this new escapade, I decided to start with a good night of sleep and good-sized breakfast. Maybe not the smartest choice to have a lump of food in your gut before you go running, but what did I know?

Once the race started, I was determined to show the naysayers and myself what I could do. I put one foot forward and then the other. I ran and I ran, and then I ran some more. Compared to skating and gliding across the ice, running is like working your butt off in agonizing slow motion. My skating legs were strong, my thighs muscular from keeping a low stance on the ice, but that day, each stride became more painful and the hot air in my lungs made me feel as though I was on fire.

Many of the other runners pulled ahead of me, and somewhere along the line, I pulled even with a man carrying a long white stick with a red stripe across the bottom. I couldn't believe what I was seeing. What the—yes, that was a walking stick for the blind. This guy was legally blind, and he was running a marathon! And he had been ahead of me! Now there was no way I was going to let a blind guy beat me in a marathon. Much like how I recall from the television show Star Trek, when Scotty would always find a reserve and pull Captain Kirk and the Enterprise out of a seemingly impossible, dismal situation, I reached deep inside, and somewhere within my ego, I found a renewed source of motivation.

I partnered up with that very determined, amazing man, and I ran alongside him through kilometer after kilometer of that grueling course. I huffed, and I puffed, and right after the last bend in that marathon, within sight of the finish line, I abandoned my wingman and pulled ahead of that blind guy, putting as much distance between us as I could muster. Much to the surprise of Gary and his wallet, I finished that marathon! And I finished it ahead of the blind guy! I raised a good amount of funds for the charity that day and went home with a body that was sorer than it had been after any game I ever played. I suffered for two weeks afterward. Needless to say, that was my *first and last* marathon.

Another noteworthy event that comes to mind is an unusual exhibition game I played with the Jets alumni one year at a penitentiary in Winnipeg. Turns out there were a lot of inmates who played hockey, and they asked the alumni to play a game with them to boost the inmates' morale. What could go wrong, right?

One fine Sunday afternoon found us walking into the prison, going through inspection, getting clearance, and then entering the inner portions of the giant facility. When we made it in, we were there among the inmates who were watching television. We suited up and made our way to the outdoor rink where we warmed up along with the inmates. Yes, even some of the prisons in Canada have ice skating rinks inside them. As I mentioned, it was a fine Sunday afternoon, but a cold one, and the crisp air added a sharpness to the already tense atmosphere.

Not knowing quite how to interact with these fellas, at the faceoff, I asked the wing who was playing against me what he was in for. His response was simply, "Murder." I got chills on the chills I already had and wondered what I was up against, questioning my sanity for agreeing to be there. The game went fine. It was quite fun, as some of the inmates were very good players. Afterward, we all got together and ate. The food there was very good. Missing was the customary post-game beer. No beer in prison, of course. I think the game was a good morale booster for the inmates and a success for the Jets alumni organization. I applaud them for participating in such an unconventional matchup.

In between all the work, the hockey, and other nonsense, like marathoning, I also had time for golf. Being members of the golf club was good for the kids, too, as they enjoyed time on the course. Although Canada is known for being cold, the spring, summer, and fall in Winnipeg are beautiful. If you ignore the occasional mildly annoying wind, the weather is fantastic.

The winters, however, become harder to ignore, as one grows older and wiser, so eventually, we would fly south as do so many others. We have many good friends from Winnipeg, and many of them have now become snowbirds. We see them here in Arizona, which is wonderful. With many friends also come the occasional tragedies that happen from time to time, and we are not immune. While we always look forward to phone calls from friends, it's always horrifying to hear of deaths and accidents. Sadly, with age, that happens more frequently. One such call came recently about the child of family friends who was in an auto accident. My only message in this is to cherish every moment, hold good people near to your heart, and treat people well.

Our life in Winnipeg was comfortable and easy, but the call of the wild was getting louder. Linda and I, with our children raised, were ready to set out on another new adventure. My aging, bruised, hockey body was also calling for a nicer climate, for warm sunshine. After much thought, consideration, anticipation, and then a roll of the dice, we set out on our next move. Florida seemed to be the place to go. We had visited there many times, had a timeshare there, and many friends from Canada were there—just like that, off we went.

Little did we know, our jaunt to Florida would bring us challenges like no other and tragedy unlike any other we had lived through.

The Beaudin family (1980)

Norm running a marathon on Father's Day – June 19th, 1979

Chapter Eight

FLYING SOUTH

Leaving Winnipeg was difficult. Moving to Switzerland had been a big decision, but this was much greater. I liken it to having to make the difficult decision to put an aging pet to sleep. You still love that pet with all your heart, perhaps more than ever, but you need to let him or her go. You need to make the right choice. Looking back, at times we think that perhaps we didn't make the right choice and that we should have stayed and somehow endured the cold; however most days we are happy to enjoy where we are now, and we look forward to what is ahead. With those thoughts of looking ahead, we decided in 1988 to make a bold move and head south to Florida.

It's not that we didn't like where we were; we were leaving prosperity in Winnipeg, as well as our home, our friends, and our wonderful fans. It was just that, as a family, we're not afraid to be adventurous, and we're interested in exploring new cultures—not as outsiders, but by completely immersing ourselves in them, which makes for an interesting life. We had spent a great deal of time in Florida and had vacationed there for weeks at a time, enjoying the beautiful beaches and warmer weather. We had fallen in love with it.

Things don't always go off without a hitch, however, and this was no exception. Leaving Winnipeg and getting our green cards didn't happen overnight. Today, I hear stories about how people just walk over our porous border and say, "here I am, take me, I want my education paid, my healthcare paid," and they are met with little or no resistance. We chose the proper way to migrate to a new country, though. We gathered all the paperwork that was required; we had to fly to Calgary twice to finalize things; we had to prove we had this and that; show a history of what we had done and accomplished; and prove that we were financially stable, healthy citizens able and willing to work. We were fortunate in that one of our sons is American, so he was able to sign for us and assist us in the process. In all, we spent in the ballpark of $5,000 to obtain our green cards, but we are proud Americans. We have learned the history of the country and continue to enjoy traveling around and learning about this great land.

In August of 1988, Linda and I flew from Canada to Fargo, North Dakota and went through customs there before flying to Florida later that day. We didn't have our belongings yet, as the moving van was packed and waiting in Canada for the green light to move all of our furniture and things into the States.

In 1984, we had invested in a condo in Florida with a couple of partners, and the condo was unoccupied at the time, so we were able to settle there until we found a more permanent place to live. Once we got things in order, it was time for me to once again hit the streets and find a job. At that time, the business of selling bottled water was beginning to boom, so I attended a week-long seminar on the topic and was hired. I was thinking it was along the lines of the liquor sales I did in Canada, and how bad could it be, right? The company gave me leads, and after the week of training, I hit the road with my attaché case and my kit. I made a couple of calls, and you know what? It wasn't like selling liquor in Canada. I had spent a week training, and in less than a day, I knew that was not the job for me. It was terrible. I don't know what I was thinking. Selling water doesn't make people happy like selling them liquor—so, back to job hunting.

One day when I was at Lechmere, a subsidiary of Montgomery Ward based out of Boston, I was talking to the manager of the Clearwater store and mentioned that I was looking for work. We sat down in his office, and he asked me what I would like to do. At the time, I was almost forty-seven years old and trying to get established again in a new area. I'd rather be working at a minimum wage job and putting together a new venture than sitting around doing nothing. We talked about a lot of things and different positions available in the company, and he said to me that because of my age and the fact that maybe I had a little more experience than others, instead of starting me out at $4.65 an hour, he would start me at $4.85 an hour selling things in the sports department. Can you imagine? Going from playing in the NHL to making $4.85 an hour? But that was fine with me, it was a new start. There were signs that maybe that wasn't for me, if I had only heeded them, but I was too focused on getting out of the house and making something happen to pay attention.

One of the first signs was on that first day work. Since we only had one car, Linda was dropping me off, and as soon as I stepped out of the car, like a nervous kid on his first day of school with my lunch box in hand, another car nearly side-swiped us and almost wiped me out. I mean it was coming at me like Eddie Shack trying to clear the track. Luckily, they swerved at the last second and missed me, or I would have been gone. Gone. Just like that. Flattened. When I made it into the store, I was still quite shaken, and the staff was probably a little confused over why I was so elated to start my first day at this new job. I was happy just to still be alive!

Working in the sports department was a natural for me; I was selling up a storm. After about a month, the assistant manager asked me if I would like to move into a commission sales position in the electronics department. Bigger money sounded good to me, so I jumped over into that department, despite not knowing much about the latest in communications, which I still do not to this day. I started selling televisions, camcorders—you name it, I sold it. Every time I sold something, the key was to sell the associated warranty, which I was pretty good at, being a fan of warranties myself. You see, when you move every few months, things stop working, and things get broken. Those warranties are mighty handy documents. Anyway, things were going great there until about four or five months later when the store manager called a meeting. Everyone was called in, and they told us they were shutting down our beautiful store. Just like that, I was back out on the street.

In the meantime, Linda had found a job working for a doctor as a receptionist, and we had found a nice condo right on a golf course in Clearwater, so some things were coming together. We ordered our belongings to be shipped out of storage from Winnipeg and settled in our new place around February of 1989. While our son Greg was visiting, we ended up talking to a mutual friend, Terry Hashimoto, for whom Greg had worked in the past, and Terry knew of a restaurant that was available to be taken over by a new proprietor. Terry was a golf pro, working at a course called the Golf and Sea Club just south of Tampa. It was a very nice resort area, and the restaurant happened to be vacant. It all sounded good to me, so I said to myself, "There's a new experience, let's go for it." I had never run a restaurant before or done anything like that, but I can cook a little, and I like food, so it seemed like another good fit.

We jumped headfirst into our new venture. The Penske Group owned the course, and I signed the contract right away to start running Sand Traps Restaurant. It was a beautiful area, right on the bay, but that beauty would soon hit me right between the eyes. I had to be cooking breakfast in the wee hours of the morning so that golfers with the earliest tee times were done eating before they hit the course. With the half hour driving time, I was getting up *very* early. That comes a little easier for me now, but back then, it was not an hour at which I wanted to be waking up. I just didn't fully function at that time of day. I still don't skate early mornings, never have.

I recall one time I asked a table of customers how they would like their eggs, which they ordered over easy. I went back into the kitchen and broke some of the yolks, so I went back and asked the customers if they had ordered scrambled. We all had a laugh, and thankfully they were pleasant people, but that was one of the challenges I faced early on.

Running the restaurant was a family affair. Our daughter Carrie moved down from Winnipeg, and when she wasn't attending dental hygiene school, she would make the drive over and help out where she could, often on the cart, selling items to golfers. During that time, Carrie reunited with one of her childhood friends from Winnipeg, whom she hadn't seen in years—Bobby Hull's son Blake, who was working as an assistant golf pro at the course. Their friendship blossomed into something more, and soon they were a couple. The next thing you know, they were married. That was an exciting time for all of us, two hockey families united and looking forward to the future.

Speaking of two families, it was during our time in Florida that Linda got a call that came out of nowhere, and the story tells like something out of Hollywood. I was at home after having kidney surgery and the phone rang. We always try to answer the phone before it switches the call over to the answering machine, so she rushed to answer the call. On the other end was a schoolmate of hers from Canada, Rita Ray. Rita explained that she was working for a government adoption agency called Adoption Canada and that the agency was trying to get a hold of Linda. Curious, Linda phoned the agency right away and found out that the agency had a request from someone who was attempting to get in touch with Linda and claimed to be a relative.

Linda was raised as an only child, and we couldn't piece together what was happening until Linda talked to a woman who turned out to be Linda's biological sister! After all those years of seeing my family and yearning to be a part of a big family, Linda found out that she was actually one of thirteen children born to a woman in Canada, who was turning eighty years old. Linda had been put up for adoption during the war years as her mother was struggling to raise the older children she already had. At the request of Linda's biological mother, the sister had contacted the adoption agency and after the death of Linda's adoptive parents, the adoption agency agreed to speed up the location process because of the Linda's mother's declining health.

There are enough details to the story to fill a book of its own, but I'll skip to the happy ending and say that Linda reunited with the mother she never knew she had and united with her ten siblings who were still living, as two had passed. Linda is a beautiful, younger image of her mother, and I know her world became so much more complete even though she never knew there was a gap. There were instant relationships born, and the siblings remain in close touch to this day. We even flew down the family for one of our charity tournaments.

Sometime later, I think it was in 1991 or so, the Gulf War was on in the Middle

East and Terry, Blake, and I saw the need to put together a charity tournament to help out the Gulf War families. It's never easy to have a family member deployed, and even harder to have them return hurt. I could only imagine it was a challenge greater than any I had faced, and I wanted to help in any way I could.

We organized the tournament, hired a real chef, assembled foursomes, and brought in celebrities. Blake naturally brought in his dad, we had Phil Esposito, some football players, and other hockey players. We paired them up with participants, totaling about 200 golfers. Uh-oh, that meant food for 200 plus people. I was getting better at running the restaurant, but that was *way* out of my league, so I turned over everything to the chef we hired. Things were looking good, but as goes life, there were some bumps in the road ahead of us that day.

On the day of the tournament, Linda accidentally woke up at four in the morning and got everyone up thinking it was go-time. It wasn't, but everyone got up and got ready before they realized they were hours ahead of schedule. Oops! Two of our other kids, Nadine and Greg, had come in to help with the tournament, and they were exhausted before they went to bed only to be awakened prematurely. They made it to the tournament that day, but they were quite tired for the event.

The Lord gave us beautiful weather for our golf day, and we had a great meal planned including steaks, potatoes, and dessert. We planned to cook the steaks on the barbeque, but somehow, we must have overloaded that thing because the fire went out. Of course, there's no way to cook on a BBQ without fire, so we were in a bit of a pickle. Eventually, we got the coals re-stoked, and between that and the kitchen, we were able to prepare a satisfactory meal for our crowd. It wasn't great, but our patrons were. With the great support of Bobby, Phil, and the others, we had a successful auction and raised a lot of money to give to the Gulf War wives.

That was pretty much the highlight of my restaurant career. Summers in Florida slowed down, as did restaurants, when the snowbirds went back home for the season. When our contract was up that August, we said goodbye to the restaurant business and the grueling hours we were putting in there. Linda was still working at her stable job at the doctor's office, but I was on to the next adventure.

Sales had been good to me over the years, and one of my golfing friends that I had worked with at Lechmere was working at Sears in Clearwater, and he asked me to join him. That job sounded like something I could do, so I applied and got the job selling automotive things, like tires, batteries, parts, and of course, warranties. I was working there for a short time when I threw a tire up on a rack and tore something in my shoulder. All those years in hockey, pounding that rubber puck back and forth across the ice, sometimes even eating a puck or two, and what does me in but an even bigger round piece of rubber.

After I had surgery to repair the damage I had done, it seemed like I should pursue something a little safer, something like hockey. I hadn't played since I was in Winnipeg, but there was a new arena being built around the same time that the Tampa Bay Lightning were coming into the picture. Interest in hockey was building in Florida.

Phil Esposito co-founded the franchise, and we were not only excited to see the Lightning in Florida, but also eager to help grow the sport there. Our son Dave, who was teaching in Canada at the time, came to visit us, and because of his success playing hockey at Ohio State, he ended up getting a job as the hockey director of the Tampa Bay Skating Academy.

My arm was still in a sling when I was hired as Dave's assistant, but soon it was time to step back on the ice. It was a momentous occasion for me. It felt so good to be back. After about a year, Dave went to open a rink in New York, so I became the new hockey director for the academy. The job included hosting clinics for adults, running the programs, and coaching the kids—things that I loved doing. When I started, there weren't many teams, but with about six months of development efforts, I created, I think, forty-four adult teams. The rink was flourishing. I ended up doing that for about ten years, and those years flew by.

Being on the ice and getting the exercise that my body craved put me back in great shape physically. No more slinging tires for me. Or slinging hash. Hockey was where I belonged. Was Linda happy to see me back on the ice? Yes and no. The competition can be difficult to watch, and I think she still worries greatly about me getting hurt, although she allows me to be out there without a complaint. She's such a supportive woman, such a rock of sanity and stability for our family, while still finding ways to keep her sense of humor intact and sharing it with those around us. I was playing in an A-league (very competitive level) and was doing a lot of work at the rink off the ice, staying until the last games were finished, which was often after midnight. I was well appreciated by the back-office at the rink, to be sure.

One thing my family and I do more than change jobs is move a lot. No kidding, right? One time, we had sold a home and had rented another. I had brought a load of goods to the new rental house and left it there, including a wooden snake I had received from my son Greg. I left the snake on the floor and went for another load. While I was gone, one of the landlords dropped by to make sure everything was in order, and when she saw the snake in the kitchen, she about lost it. To her defense, there are a lot of big creepy things in Florida, so one is always kind of on the lookout.

She fled the snake-infested house and left a hysterical message for me not to go back into the house, but I was in transit and didn't get the message. She then proceeded to call her husband who was a firefighter. As the fire crew was en-route to save the day, she must have called everyone else she knew to tell them about the giant snake. When I arrived back at the home to the crowd in the yard, the fire department had just arrived, and it took everything in me to quell my laughter enough to tell them it was a fake snake. The fire chief made me promise not to share the story, but it's too good not to tell here.

Snakes being the slithery, slinky, sneaky things they are, that same snake found its way to a family friend, Wayne LaRue, who is petrified of anything snaky. Wayne was so fortunate to have found it gifted to him in his car. Still others have received the snake in their hockey bag, so beware. Somehow, Mr. Snake always finds his way back to us to be set upon another unsuspecting soul.

Those were good times. As I sit here and mull the past, some negative aspects of my life come to mind, but it seems I do a pretty good job at shutting them out. While we were in Florida, Linda had a stroke and suffered a series of related complications, but we don't tend to dwell on that, so it doesn't come to mind very often. Our kids have gone through difficult times, as everyone does, but we focus on the good.

We also squeeze in some vacation time here and there, but even what should be a docile vacation can bring some excitement to the Beaudin clan. One morning in Honolulu, Linda was enjoying sleeping in, but I wanted to get in some morning exercise so I ventured out alone into the water. Somehow, the tide was going out, and I was swept right with it. There was an undertow and powerful waters that just pulled and pulled. As much as I fought against them, I couldn't make my way back to shore. I knew how to get out of the undertow, which I did successfully, and I stayed on the top of the water until things calmed down. By then, I was hundreds of yards out from shore, beyond yelling distance, and I knew I was in trouble. I did the only thing I could do, I stayed calm until the waters smoothed out enough for me to make it back to shore. I remember saying, I would never run another marathon again, but I guess I left out swimming one. I'm lucky to have survived that little workout. Vacations can be dangerous!

During our time in Florida, it was nice to be working with our kids. As I mentioned, Carrie worked with me, she finished college, and got married to Blake Hull. When it was time to enlist the assistance of a celebrity for another charity hockey game at the Tampa Bay Skating Academy, I once again turned to Bobby Hull. I organized a game, the Tampa Bay Lightning against us old guys, to raise money for our youth hockey programs. The kids are always in need of equipment and funds to build the program, so it was an important cause for me. Bobby came in, and although he wasn't able to play at the time, he signed autographs for hours and hours and brought in a great deal of money for the cause. I think there were about a thousand people at the game, so we raised several thousand dollars for the program. We were able to buy goalie equipment, which is very costly; we bought sticks, helmets, and whatever we could to round out the stock that we had. This enabled so many kids to play who otherwise would not have been able to afford the necessary equipment.

One thing that has always stuck with me, which I learned early on from Bobby Hull and was reinforced by Arnold Palmer, was to always sign my name legibly. I have seen Bobby take countless hours to sign items for fans and to take the time to do it well, with pride. I remember Bobby having beautiful handwriting. I am reminded of the Declaration of Independence, and the beautiful signatures on that document. The pride and precision with which those strong men signed their name will always stick with me, and I always do my best to sign items with a neat signature, showing my gratitude for the attention.

Those were good times. We liked Florida, other than the pests, like snakes and gators—but according to Linda, "they're not bad, you just learn to deal with them, and you drive quickly through certain areas." We had great friends there, Linda liked her job, and we were feeling better being out of the cold weather in Canada. We used to have a lot of parties, all kinds of parties: holiday parties, theme parties, parties just to party. Those good times would come to be shattered however, shattered by one single phone call.

The Florida golf club (1991)

Norm's work briefcase (1991)

Norm working at his Florida desk (~2002)

Golfing in Florida (~2004)

Chapter Nine

HELPING CARRIE THROUGH HOCKEY

It's the call that every parent fears. The message began with the voice on the other end telling us that they were calling from St. Luke's Hospital in St. Louis. We were still removing our sweaters after enjoying a beautiful evening out. We listened with disbelief, that January 2nd of 1996, curiosity melting into dread before we even heard the stoic voice close the call by telling us that we should get to St. Louis as soon as possible to see our daughter Carrie.

Carrie and Blake had moved to St. Louis a couple of years before, as he got a job working for his brother there and Carrie had finished her education as a dental hygienist. It was easy for her to get established there in her new career. We saw them as often as possible and knew they were healthy, at least we assumed so, so we weren't expecting the news we were about to receive.

One first thinks of a car accident, especially when something tragic happens on a party night, but this was going to be different. When the initial diagnostics were finally complete, we knew that Carrie had suffered a brain aneurysm. She was to be in surgery for many hours, so we were able to take time to quickly pack a couple of bags of necessities before we headed out the door for the airport.

We got there the following day, and in the meantime Dave, Nadine, and Greg arrived because we didn't know if our sweet Carrie was going to live or not. It was touch and go. To arrive and see your baby in the ICU, in a coma, is not something any parent wants to experience, but at least she was alive. We had hope. Never did I ask God, "Why did this happen." I just tried to stay positive and ask God for the strength to deal with the matter. When I had returned to Winnipeg from Switzerland, I had become a member of the Knights of Columbus to get involved in the community and help the unfortunate, never thinking that I would be the one asking for prayer.

Watching one of your children suffer is an unimaginable pain, one that can't be numbed with a shot or repaired with stitches. It's a pain that lingers, and you can't push it out and revive your happiness with smelling salts like you do in hockey. There isn't anything you can do, no stops to make, no goal you can force, no one you can retaliate against to even the score. Physical pain is tough, but the pain of watching your child hurt is much more real—indescribable, really. It grips every cell of your body with an unrelenting hold and doesn't let go. I got hurt bad in hockey but nothing compared to this, and all we could do was wait. Wait and pray.

A week later, after enduring a long surgery on the stem of her brain, Carrie wasn't coming out of her coma, and we had prepared ourselves for the worst. Nadine phoned an old friend of hers who is a very popular singer in Canada and Europe to tell him about what had happened to Carrie, and a few days later we received a tape containing three songs that he had written and recorded just for Carrie. We put the music on in the ICU, and when she heard Roch Voisine's mesmerizing voice, we witnessed one of those miracles that one usually only hears about on the news or in church. Carrie responded to his voice! She came out of the coma!

Hallelujah! Our prayers were answered! About three or four days later, Carrie was talking. She was out of bed and walking, and we were celebrating her recovery. Linda stayed to assist Carrie in her recovery, but I went back to Florida to go to work. A few days later, while the doctor was on vacation, Carrie was making great progress, and the medical staff decided she was ready for some physical therapy. They took her downstairs with her sister, and as our miracle patient was exercising, she collapsed again, right there in Nadine's arms. That was it, the aneurysm ruptured, and a river of blood surged through her brain, wreaking havoc that would change us all forever.

My dad had died of a brain aneurysm in 1970, and two weeks before he died, he held Carrie in his arms. We have a picture of them together, so happy. Then, there she was, laying in a hospital with the same thing. Back in a coma, one stroke, two, three, four strokes. Linda was still there in St. Louis with her all that time, living with whomever she could. Brett Hull was there and so supportive. We were very thankful.

About three months later, Carrie was ready to be discharged from the hospital, not having made much progress. We had a friend in Tampa who was a nurse, so we decided that we would move Carrie to Florida where we were, as there was nothing left holding her to St. Louis. As we were checking out, the discharge people asked me how I would like to pay the bill. I asked them how much it was, and as I reached for my wallet, they told me it was about $750,000. I nearly had a stroke of my own!

I couldn't pay that. I don't know how Carrie's insurance was structured; I didn't have any of that information; I wasn't her husband or her guardian. It was out of my hands. All I could do was care for her from there forward.

Carrie made the flight to Florida with the nurse on an ambulatory plane, and we brought her home, hoping for brighter days. The universe had other plans, though, and even though she was well-equipped at home with us, with a nice hospital bed and everything the medical personnel told us we would need, she suffered another stroke. Back in the hospital for about another six months. How much can one person take? She had pressure on the brain, so they had to insert a shunt. Procedure after procedure, she would improve and relapse and begin the same cycle over again. In the meantime, Linda was back at work, we had one car, and we would go to see Carrie in the hospital in shifts. It was a nightmare for all, still not knowing if she would even live. She was totally paralyzed, couldn't talk, and couldn't eat.

From the hospital, she was moved into a physical therapy facility for about a month, but then it was time for her to come home with us again. We had a bed for her in our condo, but it was just too much for us to handle. Linda is tiny and couldn't lift her, and we were both working, trying to make ends meet under the burden of the medical bills. We had nurses coming in to help, but they weren't there 24-7, and we just couldn't physically give Carrie everything she needed. One of the nurses was so large, she couldn't even move around well herself, much less take care of Carrie.

On top of all that, Carrie was having seizures. She was taking all kinds of medications. I was having to carry her to the bathroom, to and from the car for appointments; it was no easy task. But I will say that my faith stayed with me. My faith provided strength. Not once did I question my faith. I did not deviate or ask, "Why us?" I just kept the faith and kept going, living day by day. Faith gave us hope that she would come through.

Because of the multiple calls put out for help, the fire department got to know us well, and they knew Carrie. They were able to respond to our emergencies, get her regulated, get her through her seizures, and get us all through our scariest times. One time, the big lady dropped Carrie on the floor. She had to call 911 and have the paramedics lift Carrie back into bed.

After several months of the same incidents, we decided to listen to those around us and put Carrie in an assisted living facility, which turned out to be nothing more than an old folks' home. Every morning at six, my buddy and I would go visit Carrie to feed her. She wasn't a candidate for an old folks' home, but there were no indigent care facilities in the area, so they accepted her. Some mornings, I would go there and the bed would be dirty; sometimes she hadn't been changed or fed; it was terrible. Carrie still wasn't eating on her own.

In what seemed to be another one of those divine interventions, one day I happened to strike up a conversation with someone who turned out to be a dietician. I was coaching her son in hockey, and she suggested that I try feeding Carrie some Italian Ice. It seems that the cold, sweet food sometimes stimulates trauma patients to the point where they begin to eat again. What was there to lose? I decided to give it a try. As soon as Carrie tasted the sweet dessert, she puckered and swallowed. I gave her some food, then a little spoon of the Italian Ice, and suddenly she started to eat. At one point, she was down to eighty-four pounds, but she's put that back on and more.

During her stay in that convalescent home, there was no therapy provided, so I was bringing her to another place three times a week. They donated their time and worked with her arms and legs as much as possible, but after about three months of that, we couldn't do it any longer. We had to find a better solution.

Throughout it all, she was improving, and there were bright spots. One time, Dave and Linda went to visit her, and Dave thought Carrie needed to spend some time outside. Linda couldn't lift her, but Dave could, so he placed her in Linda's car, and he followed as they drove toward their chosen vista.

Only those who were around to watch TV ads in that era will get this, but it seemed that while she was in the home, Carrie had been watching some TV because as Dave pulled up next to Linda's car, Carrie suddenly started fiddling with the door. Linda panicked, thinking she was trying to get out. When Carrie finally found the button that controlled the window, she rolled the window down, looked at Dave, and said, "Pardon me, do you have any Grey Poupon?"

The humor was still there. It was hysterical, and the relief was tremendous.

However, the comic relief was infrequent, and eventually we had to decide on her future. Linda and I couldn't take care of Carrie as she needed, and we weren't able to find a care facility that would take her and meet her needs. She was still improving, and the facilities available wouldn't provide her with the therapy she needed, so we made a very difficult decision to start looking elsewhere for her to live.

In the meantime, one Sunday morning I went to church. I was sitting in the pew when out of the blue, I started to bleed from my nose. It got really bad, so I got up to go to the back of the church and passed out along the way. Someone called an ambulance, which took me to the hospital, and by the time I got there, the bleeding had stopped. They ran a bunch of tests and told me that I was fine. I felt good after that until I got to church the next week and the priest came up to me and said, "I thought you were dead." Just like that. Deadpan, no, "Glad to see you're okay, what can we do," nothing. Just, "I thought you were dead." I guess all the stress was taking a toll on me.

Thankfully, there were breaks in the seriousness, such as when a fan from the past tracked me down, which they still do, and it always brightens my day. In 1964, while playing in Memphis, I occasionally had fans ask me for an autographed stick. It wasn't easy to give out sticks, but this one guy in particular seemed to be a loyal fan, so after one game, I called him over and asked him if he still wanted a stick. He was elated. I signed the stick and wrote out his name: Vic Erdelyan. He was a very passionate hockey fan. Fifty years later, I received a package in the mail and not knowing what was in it, I opened it to find out that Vic had passed away and he had left the stick with his friend, who found my address in Tampa and shipped the stick back to me. There it was, a Northland Pro stick, bearing the words "To Vic Erdelyan," with my signature. It certainly was a surprise package, needless to say, and it was quite amusing to see such a straight blade, kind of a glimpse into the past.

But the stresses of the present were always at the forefront with occasional breaks of relief. Somewhere along the way, we met a gentleman who said he would take Carrie in, give her therapy, give her what she needed, and keep her there with about twelve other patients. Even at $12,000 a month, it sounded like a good idea since we couldn't give her what she needed. So, we moved her in and set out to find a way to make it work.

As a family, we decided to do something about our financial plight and the burden that taking care of Carrie was putting on all of us, knowing that we wanted to get her the best care possible. Greg and Dave created the F.O.C.U.S. Foundation (Friends Of Carrie Unite and Support). With a lot of help from friends and family, we held several golf tournaments in Florida and one in British Columbia, Canada, to raise funds for her care.

We had been fortunate to be surrounded by caring, helpful people who had arranged charity tournaments and fundraisers, and we had funds to care for her for a while. So many people in Florida and Canada gave generously of their time to help Carrie's cause. Roch Voisine, our friend who is a singing sensation in many parts of the world, helped. Roch has such a great voice. You'll be doing yourself a favor if you listen to some of his music. The Lightning were instrumental in raising funds for us. This is what I mean about hockey family. We are there for each other through thick and thin. Vincent Lecavalier, a first round draft pick, helped at one tournament. The Hanson Brothers were instrumental in helping us raise a lot of money in several golf tournaments and hockey games which we had in Winnipeg. Dave and his friend Peter Young organized a hockey game in Winnipeg Arena. Through different celebrities, like the Winnipeg Jets Alumni who played against the Pondkings Clan (a hockey-playing group of twenty Beaudins) in a match-up in the Winnipeg Arena and the Flying Fathers who played in another game that drew about 12,500 fans, our Carrie was helped tremendously. We also held a Saturday night dinner, which was a huge success and raised a lot of money for Carrie's cause. Dean Gunnarson, who is a Houdini-type performer, put on a great act, and one of the pitchers from the New

York Yankees was there.

My one regret is that I did not contact Bobby Hull to talk to him about what was going on or give him a chance to participate, as I had seen his consistent generosity throughout the years. But at times, men's egos get in the way of logical thinking, and if I could turn back the clock, I would have worked to bridge the gap that had grown between us since Carrie's accident. We simply let time and distance come between us, which we shouldn't have. My message is, if there is a phone call you know you need to make, make it. Tomorrows are limited and not guaranteed.

After several months in that facility, it was clear that it was time to do something different. The expenses were too much to bear, and our Carrie was not getting the care she needed. Our son Greg, who was living in Vancouver, met a man there who, when he learned of Carrie's situation, agreed to take her into his facility in Canada for $5,000 a month, which was a lot better than $12,000 a month. It seemed they would give her better care than she was getting, and she would be near Greg with whom she was very close. Since at that time she still didn't have the ability or cognition to make such decisions, we had to make the difficult decision to let her go. While there have been some hiccups, it was the right move to make.

One of the incidents was when one of the guys she knew fairly well just up and died in the bathroom, and she found him there. That's not what you want your disabled daughter to experience, that's for sure. With disability comes depression, and many of the patients there were self-medicating addicts using cocaine and other drugs, so it wasn't the greatest facility. Although it seems there are problems everywhere, even though Carrie seems to be a magnet for bad luck.

One time after a doctor's appointment, the transporters dropped Carrie off, put her in the elevator, watched the doors close, and left her alone in the elevator to get into her apartment. Well, they put her in backwards, and the buttons were behind her, so when the doors closed, she was stuck. All she knew to do was to phone us in Florida. We couldn't coach her out of her situation, so we tried to call the home. Well, the on-site workers were busy with their own things (often happens after hours), and they didn't pick up the phone. So, we resorted to calling emergency services in Vancouver (from Florida), and after a couple of hours, Carrie was freed from the elevator.

There have been many blessings along the way, however. Carrie has met a good friend, also disabled. He's French, and he had recognized her name and gravitated toward her. He had his own apartment, and they ended up moving in together and taking care of each other, quite a nice arrangement.

Another divine blessing came our way when Carrie's friend's van was getting very dilapidated, and it just so happened that I was in Florida giving a young man private hockey lessons. He was from a well-to-do family in Clearwater, and one day when I was talking with the father, I told him about Carrie and that I needed to raise funds to buy her a van. He said, "Funny you talk about a van. My dad just died, He's got a beautiful van, and you can have it." The van was beautiful, immaculate, had all the features needed for Carrie and her friend, so we shipped it to Vancouver, and they were set. Things were stable and looking up, so what do Linda and I decide to do? You got it. Make a change.

At that time, it was about 2001, Carrie was in Vancouver, we missed her, and decided that we were going to become part of the road-tripping set. We bought a motorhome—beautiful thing, all the creature comforts one could want. We quit our jobs, sold our house, put some of our stuff in storage, sold the rest, and hit the road.

It was May when we loaded up and headed west, first to Jacksonville, Florida. When we had told the kids we were retiring and going to set out to travel, they had sent us a bunch of gift cards, hotel vouchers, and things of the like—and it's a good thing, because when we stopped there in Jacksonville, after a day in that coach, there was no way I was going to hunt down a place to park, hook up to facilities, and sleep in that little metal tube. Nope, not gonna happen. So, we parked in a hotel parking lot and got a room: a nice, wide room with no wheels that didn't rock with each step.

From there, we drove to see friends in other parts of Florida, New Orleans, Missouri, all over, and wherever we went, we would stay with friends or in a hotel. We used our timeshare hotels, and eventually decided we needed to head toward Vancouver. Well, I don't know what it was that flipped the switch, but partway through Texas, I said, "That's it, I'm turning around." And I did. I was just not cut out for life in a motorhome. We drove home to Florida, even though we didn't have a home there anymore. We used up our timeshare credits and moved into a condo we had bought for our son Dave years before. We never slept a single night in that motorhome.

Soon, however, we got tired of living with Dave—and he with us, I'm sure—and we had to find ourselves our own place. Kids. Can't live with them, can't live without them. There we were in Florida, no home, no car, no jobs. So, once again, I hit the streets looking for work. Linda was pretty upset with me, so she made her way to Canada and spent time with family there. Luckily, I got a call from the owner of a hockey arena in Oldsmar, Florida who needed someone to run their pro shop. With this perfect timing, even though I was computer illiterate, I could sell, so I took it over in September of 2001.

During that time, I ended up having kidney trouble and had to have surgery. I had two stents put in; one of them I later had taken out while I was awake, not frozen or anything, just awake. That was terrible, but I was able to make it to Greg's wedding in Canada. The years of stress wore on me, and I spent time in and out of hospitals, and for anyone who knows hockey players, it's the last place we want to be, so it was another tough part of my life.

Eventually we found a new home, got a car, got settled in, and got the shop going well. In fact, we decided to take on yet another shop in Bradenton, Florida. Nothing like another move, right? Things did go well, and with Dave around to help, both shops were running smoothly. I was back on the ice running clinics, working with kids and adults there, and we were content. As content as we nomads could be.

During that time, I also hit my first and only hole-in-one at Stonybrook Golf Course in Florida. I was with Phil Roberto from St. Louis, he played with the Canadiens, too, and we were with one other guy. It was a beautiful day, perfect weather for golf. The first four holes were good, and on the fifth, I teed off last at 149 yards out. I hit the ball perfectly. A golfer knows immediately if he hit the ball right, and I knew it was good. We watched it going and going and we all saw it drop and then just disappear. Wow!

It was somewhat anticlimactic, though, as the course was under renovation, and there was no clubhouse, just a trailer. We went back and told the pro, but he didn't seem too excited, and that was it. No fanfare—but I did it.

I played with friends, and it seemed to make sense to work with friends. I hired a guy from my hometown area, Regina, Saskatchewan. He had been living in Florida with his wife, and he knew business well. Having him there gave Linda and me time to go see Carrie when we could and enjoy life in Florida. We hired more people; one guy could sell anything, so it was going well; we even hired his kid. Until, about six months later, a customer came to me and told me that the young guy needed to be watched, that this customer had seen the kid trying to sell another customer a stick for $100 cash. That stick should have been $250, but the kid was selling off our inventory on the side and pocketing the cash for himself! I decided to run a little sting operation just to make sure, and sure enough, the skates that I had marked were found to be sold offsite on this kid's own website.

I had no choice but to tell his father, which was so difficult. I wish things could have been different, but the dad repaid what the kid had stolen, and they agreed to work it out between each other, which was fine with me. There were other similar incidents, a kid doing the same thing, fired him, and called the police. I hired another kid because I knew his father, who was a golf pro, and darn it if we didn't catch that kid on camera letting his buddies in and letting them walk out with our merchandise without paying for a thing. Unbelievable. I just couldn't conceive the lack of morality in that many people. To say that I was discouraged would be a monumental understatement.

After that, I hired a hockey friend, who I figured would be a good employee. Only he had demons of his own, and one time when Linda and I went to Vancouver, I checked the bank account only to see that no money was going into the account. I rushed home to find the guy drunker than hell, going to work drunk, and not making the night deposits. He would just put the money in the bank bag, put the bag in his truck, and go about life like he didn't have a hoard of my cash there in his truck. Unfortunately, I had to let him go, too, which is very difficult when it's a friend. I started thinking that perhaps I just wasn't cut out for the retail business and that we needed to make a change.

That's when the Lord stepped in and made a change for me, in about 2006 or 2007. The real estate crisis changed everything. Florida was hit hard, bankruptcies everywhere, including the arena our main shop was in. We had been doing so well that we had bought a big house, lots of big, beautiful furniture, and suddenly we were struggling to hang on. We had about $300k in stagnant, depreciating inventory that we had to move. We shut down that store, then the second store, and took everything back to the first store, but it was a fight to keep that lone store afloat until finally, it would float no more.

Until one goes through unimaginable tragedy, one cannot really appreciate all that comes along with the scene. I couldn't eat; I couldn't sleep; I'm sure I wasn't too much fun to be around, as my whole world was collapsing around me. Thankfully, though, Carrie was doing well in Vancouver with Greg there as well, and Linda and I sat down to regroup. What were we going to do?

From left to right: Greg, Norm, and Dave

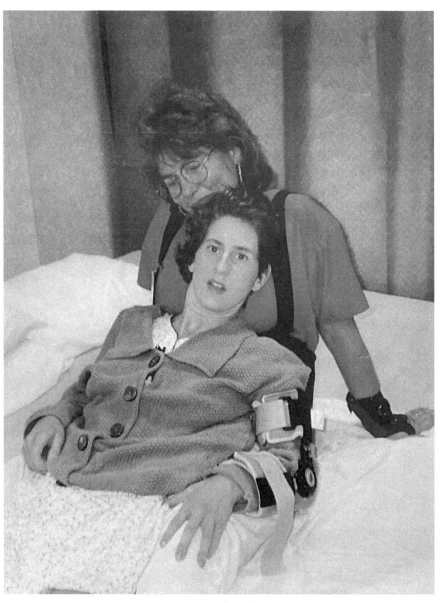

Carrie (1997)

Chapter Ten

THERE'S HOCKEY IN THE DESERT, TOO

For Norm and Linda Beaudin, it seems that nothing billows out the sails like a fresh start. Next on the list, Arizona.

In March of 2013, we made a deal with the owner of the hockey arena in Florida to buy out our inventory. I helped him out for a few months, showing him the ropes, making it an easy transition for him. In July, we made our move. We had considered Palm Springs, but that was no good, because although I wasn't saying it, I was thinking hockey. What would we do in Palm Springs? We're young, and it's blazing hot there. It's blazing hot in Arizona, but in Arizona there is hockey—and ice. Great indoor ice. Many sheets in the Phoenix valley. The Coyotes are there. Hockey arenas and hockey programs are there. The only thing going for Palm Springs was the number of friends we had there, but Arizona seemed to be the best decision, so I put forward my best sales pitch to Linda.

We had traveled a bit and spent some time in Arizona, right by the Ice Den: the Coyotes training facility—a great venue with three sheets of ice. We had a timeshare there at the Princess. We had also spent some time in Palm Springs, and after all was said and done, Arizona got the final vote. Another thing that made the transition easy was that our current leasing company from Florida had properties in Scottsdale, close to the arena, right near where we wanted to be. So, we went to the landlord's office in West Chase, and they made the arrangements.

We chose a location near the Ice Den Scottsdale and made the preparations for our move. Staying in a rental situation seems to always work best for us. We've had such bad luck with real estate that one wouldn't believe it if they heard all the bad tales. One example is a hot development in Florida in which we invested. It was situated across from the house that we had purchased in 2006. It was a condo development, a beautiful complex right where the boats were, near the marina. There was a gorgeous restaurant, and you could have a boat pick you up and take you across the water to wherever you wanted to go.

We loved the development so much that when we learned they were building a third building about twenty stories tall, we decided to put a down payment on a unit on the fourth floor, overlooking the water. We didn't think we could go wrong, as real estate prices were going up every day, and we enjoyed condominium living. Well, we all know what happened to real estate soon after that. Prices plummeted, and Florida was one of the states hit the hardest. We were waiting for our building to break ground, but target dates came and went and nothing was happening. The group ended up going bankrupt, and we lost our whole investment. So, then we were involved in a bankruptcy lawsuit.

Times were so crazy in the United States during the real estate crash. We wanted to sell our house, but the bank couldn't even find our title. Paperwork had been transferred from lender to lender, and banks were going under left and right. Homeowners were left holding the bag. We got caught up in something we didn't understand and still do not understand to this day. Crazy times—times that would send us westward, toward the setting sun, in search of our next adventure.

It was around September 15th of 2013 that the moving company picked up our furniture. They said they would meet us in Arizona in five days. As it turned out, the truck was late, and when they finally arrived, everything was wet. Soaked through and through. Not a good way to start that new adventure, that's for sure. We dried our belongings as best we could and moved them into our new apartment in Scottsdale. We loved that location. We would go for walks on the pedestrian path and view all the local wildlife. We saw javelina and coyotes, and we felt very welcomed by everyone there—whether they be winged, four-legged, or two-legged beings.

In beautiful Scottsdale, I immediately got involved with the Knights of Columbus at St. Patrick's Catholic Church and knew we had made the right choice in where to live. I like to think that the church needs me, and I know that I need the church.

After living there for about a month or so, we got settled in, and I decided to head to the Ice Den to see what I could do there. At the time, I had no idea that an old friend, Michael O'Hearn, who had worked with the Jets years before, was the President of Coyotes Ice and running the Ice Den. It wasn't until I went there and asked to talk to the manager that I learned Mike was overseeing the place. He remembered me from Winnipeg, so we started talking hockey. What a nice surprise to see someone, a great personality, from back home! I asked if they had a clinic; he said no, and the rest was history. I built the program, and it's been going ever since. I still play there in a rec league with friends when I am in the area.

While we were living in Arizona, we got another one of those dreaded telephone calls, again involving Carrie. We were informed that Carrie had some trouble getting across a street in her wheelchair and had been hit by a bus! Her chair was tipped over, and she broke bones in her hip and leg. On top of that, she wasn't a candidate for surgery, so they tried to manage her care with pain medication, which often doesn't sit well on her stomach. Hard to get relief with an oral pill if you can't keep it down. The challenges just seem to keep on coming for Carrie, but she has a resiliency unmatched by anyone I know.

Carrie has had her personal trials, and I was to be confronted with one of my own soon after we moved to Arizona. After about three months of being in this beautiful state and doing my hockey clinic, after a routine physical check-up, I was diagnosed with prostate cancer. After several weeks of having more tests to determine the extent of the cancer and what the best course of action would be, the doctor decided I should have surgery, so on April 30th of 2014, the doctor performed the operation to remove the cancer.

After the procedure, I was bedridden for several weeks in what I can best describe as a very uncomfortable situation. Luckily, my son Greg came to the rescue and helped our situation because Linda was not driving at the time. I managed to heal and get back on the ice and do what I do best. Playing hockey, I'm sure, gave me strength to heal and get back up, going faster than I or even the doctor expected. Mind you, I did have to go to the emergency room once during my healing time, but the rest of the process was pretty much a textbook recovery. It doesn't matter how tough you are, or how in shape you think you are, go to those regular doctor visits. I am so thankful to have made it through that difficult trial surrounded by many good friends.

I have a strong kinship with many people involved in hockey in Arizona and have reconnected with people from Canada who now live in Arizona part of the year. I don't miss the cold and snow of Canada one little bit; it's just too much to handle as one gets older. I would much rather shovel sunshine than snow.

Our recent moves to Sun Lakes and subsequently Chandler, Arizona have taken me away from Scottsdale but not from the church. I still stay involved with the Knights of Columbus and do not stray from the church. We all must try and strive for salvation. I hope to get more involved and help more people through prayer. I enjoy donating my time and efforts to the Knights of Columbus. Again, I cannot deviate from my beliefs.

One big annual production that the Knights of Columbus in Scottsdale put on is a big charity event benefitting the Children's Cancer Network. I'm happy to be involved each year when I'm in the area. We are happy to receive donations to auction off from Coyotes players, such as new captain Oliver Ekman-Larsson and the previous captain, Shane Doan. Shane is such a wonderful, giving man; we are extremely fortunate here in the valley to have athletes like him to be role models to our children and to the adults, as well. At the beginning of each year, I find myself looking forward to this event in particular.

Although we move frequently, I am a creature of habit—I guess a little ritualistic. I stick with what works, I suppose. I like steak, a baked potato, veggies, and a little ice cream before a big game. When I was playing professionally, I also had an appetite for a nice nap after that good meal.

I have two cups of coffee in the morning, usually by eight or nine a.m., and no more during the day. I like a beer or two after a game, but never over-do it. I stick to my morals and be the best person I can be, day in and day out—and that feels really good inside.

Another habit (surprise!) seems to be that we are surrounded by crazy events. A recent debacle was when we were selling our townhome. Our realtor said he was sending over a construction crew to make some modifications and updates in our kitchen. I wasn't keen on the idea, but it's what he recommended, so we went along. On the scheduled morning, our doorbell rang and outside stood three guys who I was sure were pulling some sort of joke on us. They looked just like the Three Stooges, complete with giant ladders and coveralls—the whole works. Mind you, our kitchen had just a seven-foot drop ceiling, you could reach up and touch it with your hands without a ladder, but they hauled in what looked to be six-foot, eight-foot, and ten-foot ladders. But why? I guess they were emotionally attached to their ladders or something, I don't know, but those ladders came in with the guys and left with the guys, spending the time in between laying down and watching from the living room.

Partway through the first day (this job was only supposed to take a couple of hours), one of the guys asked me to bring him to the home improvement store, because he had to get more paint. More paint? For what? Our low ceiling was like an eight feet by ten feet square; you could paint it with a bottle of nail polish. Well, he explained, on the way over, the paint they had in the trunk had tipped over and spilled, while soaking his clothes that were in the trunk. The car smelled too strongly of paint to drive it—probably a fire hazard, too, I would imagine. So, I brought him to the store and got some more paint so they could finish the job. Only they couldn't finish. Instead of the measure twice, cut once rule, they seemed to follow the "measure a few times, talk about it, chat on the phone, measure some more, put up a ladder, take it down because you don't need it, measure some more, take a lunch break, measure some more, discuss, leave for the day, and finish at a later date" rule.

The next day was more of the same, only they claimed to be done. Oh, no, no, no. That ceiling had more ripples in it than a pond in a hailstorm. Not acceptable! How do we sell with a kitchen ceiling that makes you seasick? After more discussion, they agreed to come back and fix it. That last day, only one of them showed up, mumbled something about reminding him "to turn his pants" (what???). We left him alone to finish up his work undistracted. When we left for lunch, we looked at his car and understood what he had meant about having "to turn his pants." He came out and took the underwear that were stretched out on his windshield and flipped them over so the other side could dry. He said he was still trying to wash the paint out of them from the trunk incident. Oh, boy, the HOA couldn't have liked that display. Good thing we were moving!

Moves are consistent, and so is my career, at least for now. I currently teach clinics at the Ice Den Scottsdale and the Ice Den Chandler when I am there. I skate when I can in Canada—although the whole Covid-19 situation has changed the landscape a bit. I play in a Sunday league with my close friends on a team called the Pirates and cannot foresee hanging up my skates. Somehow people always track down my address and send me requests for autographs, and I respond faithfully. It is not *my* love of the sport, but it is *the fans* love of the sport that has brought me this wonderful life.

While life as a professional sports competitor can be glamorous, it can be a grueling career of hard physical work and moving, time away from family, and occasionally peppered with injury, but ours has been a good life. Knowing that I have brought joy and inspiration to people all over the world not only makes me feel good, but also reinvigorates me to keep going and keep doing well by my fellow man.

Also at this time, I am actively involved in introducing a game that is big in Europe to North America, called floorball. My son Greg is working to bring the game in a big way to people everywhere, working day in and day out to instill the game in every ice hockey player in the U.S.A. and Canada. It's a great game for off-ice training, to improve your puck-handling skills for the great game of hockey, or to just play on its own. I've heard that Wayne Gretzky will attest to that. The minute you put a Floorball stick in a kid's hand, they are glued to it and can't put it down. More challenges are in the works to evolve the game and improve every young or experienced hockey player. Many players in Europe play floorball and look at their skills. Greg hopes to work with all NHL teams to institute floorball in children's programs in schools, and hopefully, we will see it grow into recreation centers and develop individual interest as well.

Sometimes fans will ask me what I think about the evolution of the game of hockey. In addition to the off-ice changes and improvements, such as various training programs like floorball that are now available to players, over my lifetime, I have seen the leagues grow and adapt, as well. The NHL continues to improve and respond to its fanbase and players. Rules have been changed or altered from time to time, and I think most rules the NHL has changed over the years have worked for the better.

The no-touch rule on icing (shooting the puck across the center line and the opponent's goal line) has eliminated a lot of injuries. It may not seem as exciting to some folks, but it helps the defensemen a lot because it takes away some of the risk they have of high-speed chases and collisions.

I think eliminating the red line creates a more open game and more exciting play. I still think fighting in hockey is what the fans want, but tamping down the goon tactics used to injure the more-skilled players is a good thing—especially when game play speed is increasing. Players today are so fast on the ice; it's incredible.

Hitting from behind is certainly a no-no in my book. The good body-checking should always be part of the game, but I'm totally against the goons that are there to intentionally injure players or to intimidate them. Because the game has changed, especially with bigger players and the speed, the rules allowing for player protection by eliminating some of the most hazardous situations have changed the game for the better. Fans may want to watch a fight or see an extreme hit, that is, until it's their son, daughter, or favorite player, lying there in the hospital, not knowing who they are or worse. As far as the game today, I enjoy watching hockey with its speed and finesse. My television is tuned to a game whenever possible. I think the fans are watching an exciting game, and I leave each NHL game that I attend with the same exhilaration as I always have.

After being in Arizona and enjoying every minute of it, I would like to reflect on my time there. When I started my clinic with the help of Becky Conlon and Mike O'Hearn, it was instant success. The enthusiasm was great from every player—the guys and the gals. I got response from total beginners, some who had not skated for several years, and some who wanted to get back into the game. The idea was to help players get onto a team and start playing. It's so great to see players score their first goal or start coaching their son or daughter, so it's been very inspirational to see the dramatic improvements made by all players.

I also enjoy playing in the league where I can help other players improve their game. I must say, it's an honor to compete alongside the athletes I have coached and helped out. I will continue my clinic and will continue playing in the league until my shoulder pads fall apart or my body breaks down. I'm guessing the guys I play with will put their money on the pads breaking down first, as I've worn the same ones for decades. I'm an old-school guy who fixes instead of replaces. Duct tape aids in that endeavor!

Norm and John Passante

Chapter Eleven

THE HONOR TOUR

St. Louis Blues

There I was in Arizona in 2016, enjoying the hot summer—the part of the summer where you need oven mitts to turn your steering wheel if you leave your car parked outside of the garage for too long. I got home from shopping with Linda, and we noticed our phone was flashing with messages. We turned on the recorder with several messages from Joe Daley, as well as from Dave and Greg, our sons, that the Blues organization was looking for me. They had a hard time finding me because of our constant moving. They should have asked some fans because I swear some of them do better detective work than the FBI. They seem to hunt me down wherever I go, and it's always a nice surprise to hear from them. I try to always respond if they have requested an autograph, as I still feel obliged to return the good feelings fans have given me over the years.

After listening to the messages, I contacted the Blues office, and I was told Bruce Affleck, Executive Vice President of the Blues, was looking for me. I phoned him right away, and he explained to me that they were inviting the original Blues team—those who played in the first game of the Blues against the Minnesota North Stars fifty years ago—to a series of ceremonies and activities revolving around opening night that October. He explained to me what was going to happen and that I was invited to attend the reunion of the original team. I was elated. We were told to arrive on October 11th and that we would be staying at the Ballpark Hilton Hotel. What an exciting time that would be!

That October, at the airport, Linda and I met up with an old teammate, Fred Hucul, and his wife and daughter. I hadn't seen Fred since 1967! Wow, was it ever great to see him again and to find out he was living in Tucson, Arizona! We were neighbors and didn't know! And the emotional reunions continued.

When we arrived in St. Louis we were met by a limousine and greeted with open arms. It was nice to see all the activities going on where we were staying. Seeing all the players arrive and meeting them was certainly an eye-opener after fifty years. Bill McCreary who was with the team for five or six years, Larry Keenan who scored the first Blues goal—it was a great reunion and great to see him again—and Bob Plager, who's been with the team from Day One.

Good ole' Bob Plager. I remember clearly fifty years ago, when the Blues were first assembling, and I saw that he was on the team. He had hit me over the head a few years earlier, and he was a tough one to play against. I needed to make things right with him if we were going to play together, so I asked him why he had hit me over the head. He said at the beginning of the game his coach had told him to hit me so he did just that. He went over and whacked me over the head with his stick. Whacked me hard, as I was bleeding profusely and required a bit of tailor-work to get back on the ice. His explanation was good enough, I figured. Not the best way to go about it, but we were young at the time, and he just did what he was told. I was happy to be on his side of the puck. There we were, fifty years later, happy as ever just to see each other walking and talking.

The next day, we all went to a nice luncheon and were all given Blues jackets commemorating fifty years of Blues hockey. We attended the Blues practice and met all the current players. It was a great experience, seeing the new facility and the state-of-the-art dressing room compared to what we had fifty years prior. We had another great luncheon meeting with the executives, the coaches, and Ken Hitchcock, who was very gracious. That evening, October 12th, we were all greeted at the Ball Park Inn, which was quite an event. We were introduced before 3,000 fans and brought on stage with about twenty original season ticket holders.

That night, it was great to see Brett Hull again. He was so helpful to Carrie when she was going to school to get her dental hygiene certificate. We have very fond memories of those times, and I can't thank him enough for all that he did for Carrie. We had many other good times to talk about as well—talk about nostalgia. We exchanged stories between each other and were interviewed by ESPN and commentator Darren Pang, who during his career on the ice played goalie for the Blackhawks.

On October 13th, we attended the Blues game versus the Minnesota Wild—fifty years prior was the Minnesota North Stars game, which brought back a flood of memories. We were also interviewed during the game. We met the Blues owner Tom Stillman, who treated us royally and was so gracious in embracing us for being there. We were also presented with a framed original scoresheet of the first game.

What a great tribute, which I will cherish for the rest of my life and my family will be able to enjoy.

At this time, I would like to thank the St. Louis Blues organization for a wonderful week, which Linda, our friends, and I enjoyed immensely, and for making it such a memorable occasion. Thank you for making this happen and thank you to all the great Blues fans. I'll hold the memories of the games, the town, and the fans forever in my heart.

Winnipeg Jets

To continue our Honor Tour, next was with the Winnipeg Jets. They were also looking for me, but Winnipeg had a little easier time finding me because of all the friends I left there—especially Joe Daley, whom I stayed in contact with over the years. He's another very smart man, as he also regularly vacations in Arizona.

The Jets organization contacted me regarding the Heritage Classic, which would be celebrated the week of October 20th to the 23rd. Naturally, we accepted their invitation. They set everything up, sent me an itinerary with plane tickets for Linda and me to attend the Heritage Classic, and arranged for another wonderful week of touring the town as one of the team alumni.

We arrived in Winnipeg October 19th, greeted by our good friends Joe and Darlene. We spent a couple of days visiting at their house and reminiscing over our careers and the good times we had together, especially playing for the Winnipeg Jets. It was good to have some quiet time with them, because once the greater festivities commenced, it was non-stop action—just like in the good old days.

The first night we were greeted at a bar by hundreds of Jets fans. We signed autographs and met a lot of new fans, fans whom I had not seen before but who knew all about us and the original team. The function was organized in part by Peter Young and Joe Daley, and it was held at a very popular bar, The Pint. A lot of the proceeds went to a charity, the Jets Alumni Scholarship Fund, which made the event an even more enjoyable success. That was the beginning of a great weekend, to be sure.

Next, we attended the Hall of Fame luncheon, which was another momentous event, a day of honoring Bobby Hull, Anders Hedberg, and Ulf Nilsson. The Winnipeg Jets executives attended, including the CEO Mark Chipman and the Jets coaches. That was a nice gesture by the Jets, honoring all the ex-Jets and the Hall of Famers. We ended the luncheon with an autograph signing session for the great, passionate fans of the Jets. It was disappointing to not have Bobby there, but it was great to see everyone else in attendance.

Friday night was the Gala Dinner, which was attended by over 1,000 people, including all of the available Jets alumni players and the Legends of the Edmonton Oilers, represented by all the greats: Wayne Gretzky, Mark Messier, Paul Coffey, and many others. I heard that the dinner raised over a million dollars for the True North Foundation, which helps a lot of people in the Manitoba area.

Over the next couple of days, we attended the Heritage Classic games; the regular season game and the alumni game that showcased The Legends of the Jets and Oilers, which was definitely a classic. Both games were played at the football field in Winnipeg, which sold out days before to 35,000 fans—certainly a great and memorable affair. To be back in Winnipeg, to smell the same early-winter air, to feel the same cold breeze, and to see the same lovely town, all while sharing a common love for the game of hockey with all those around us: it doesn't get better than that.

I would like to thank the Winnipeg Jets for making that great week happen for us, for the fans, and for all the Jets alumni players. It was a heart-warming pleasure to go back to Winnipeg, to be a part of that great set of events, to see all the fans and players again, and to know that hockey is alive and well in the town that birthed the Winnipeg Jets.

On a more somber note, On April 6, 2018, I turned on the TV and saw multiple stories coming out about a tragic accident that happened in Humboldt, Saskatchewan, Canada. As the story unfolded, it got more interesting, but it certainly didn't sound good. Hearing about the many young people injured and killed and learning more about what happened at the intersection where a truck driver reportedly ran a stop sign and collided with a bus carrying the Humboldt Broncos hockey team was devastating. As I listened to the reporting, I heard that one of the boys killed was from my hometown of Montmartre. Holy cow, Montmartre is a small town, and this news didn't hit *close* to home; it *hit* home. I learned that the boy's name was Adam Herold, and he and his family were our neighbors; they were farmers as well. The similarities didn't stop there. Adam was sixteen, an altar boy like me, and had just gone to Regina to play for the Pats, and that is exactly what I did sixty years prior. It was like a punch to the gut, and I knew I had to do everything I could to help out this boy's family and the community.

Adam reportedly had a lot of potential to play in the NHL, such a young life taken way too soon, and the parallels to my life make me again so thankful for all of the blessings that have been bestowed upon me and make me want to work hard to help out my fellow human beings and anyone negatively affected by this tragedy. This is the legacy I want to leave behind, that of helping people and being good to people.

Soon thereafter, I got a phone call from the Regina Pats saying they were going to do a benefit and create a tournament to raise funds for the family, including

Adam's parents, Russell and Raeleen. I flew to Regina, SK and got involved as an honorary coach for one of the teams so I did my part in a small way. It was certainly a success, as I believe they raised about $100,000 that one day.

After the tournament games were completed, I sat down with Russell, Raeleen, and their daughter Erin and asked if we could have a benefit game in Montmartre, where we were from, to support the family. It wasn't just about the money; it was about getting together, showing our support, and giving each other strength to get through this tragedy.

My son Greg organized the event, and on January 26, 2019, the two teams played: the Beaudin group versus the Herold group. We got a whole bunch of memorabilia signed. Bobby Hull got involved, as well as many of the NHL teams. We had autographed jerseys, sticks, and other items, and the town of Montmartre got many items to auction off or sell.

The game was a sellout, of course; the sense of community there was unsurpassed by anything I had seen there before. There were about twenty of us playing or coaching on the Beaudin Pond Kings, including Dave and Nadine. That was the first time I had played there in sixty years, as the last time I played there was 1959, so it brought back a lot of memories. I saw a lot of my old friends, which was great, absolutely wonderful to see them there providing support for the community. It was an outstanding success, as we even got a couple of players from the Winnipeg Jets to make the six hour drive up. Mike Ford and Perry Miller who had played for the Jets came down and supported the cause. I think we raised around $40,000 dollars with the funds benefitting the entire community, including the arena.

Getting together with the family after the game and knowing that we did something to help them out was the greatest feeling, something I will never forget. However, the highlight of the day came right at the very beginning of the game. I was opposing Russell Herold, and once the puck was dropped, somehow the opposition team got the puck and started coming to our end. Right at the end of the building was a big sign with Adam Herold's name on it, and Russell scored the first goal straight-away, right under that sign. It was the highlight of the game, having Adam's dad score the first goal—a perfect start. Being able to help people in this way was worth all of the struggles along the way.

I am also so pleased with the global hockey community after learning that the GoFundMe online fundraiser raised over fifteen million dollars for the families and those affected by the tragedy. The hockey family is indeed one very large, compassionate, supportive family. The best in the world!

Just like a giant rollercoaster, with each reunion and event, you climb higher, more elated, but eventually, you must come back to Earth. Leaving each event has been very different than in the past. The ride was over. I don't know how often we will be able to return to these great communities. I saw that in my life I had gone from student to teacher and now seem to be standing back watching it all come together, watching new teachers take my place and watching the game, and life really, go on without me. No longer feeling like I have to be a tough guy, choosing rather to embrace life's ups and downs, my heart gets heavy and it becomes an emotional time for me when I have to leave all my teammates and family or leave places like Winnipeg and Montmartre and all the great fans and friends. Those fans are very passionate, and I would like to thank them all for the great support over the years. Thank you, thank you!

And with that, a toast to all of you: a heartfelt, never-ending thank you for a wonderful career. Cheers!

CHEERS!

French..............................Bon santé
German................................Prost
French Canadian..............A votre santé
Swedish...............................Skal
Finnish................................Kippis
Russian.........................Budem Zdorovi
Italian................................Saluti
Spanish...............................Salud
Egyptian............................ Fe sahetek
Czechoslovakian.....................Na zdravi
Danish................................Skol
Norwegian...........................Skol
Polish...........................Twoje zdrowie
Japanese.............................Kan pai
Hawaiian......................... A kale maluna
Ukrainian............................Dybosyia
Young, Thirsty American...Bottoms Up

Norm and Peter Young (2021)

Carrie (2021)

Norm, Nadine & Carrie (2021)

Norm watching Blues (2019)

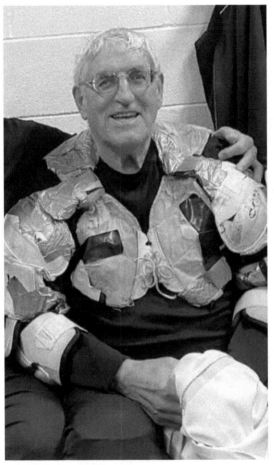

Norm with his old Original pads (2021)

Montmartre Arena Herold Benefit Event (2019)